CH00376094

Mission Praise

2

Compiled by

Peter Horrobin and Greg Leavers

WORDS EDITION

Marshall Pickering

Marshall Morgan and Scott
3 Beggarwood Lane, Basingstoke, Hants RG23 7LP, UK

Compilation copyright © 1987 Peter Horrobin and Greg Leavers

First published in 1987 by Marshall Morgan and Scott Publications Ltd
Part of the Marshall Pickering Holdings Group
A subsidiary of the Zondervan Corporation

Impression
88 87 : 5 4 3 2

ISBN: 0 551 014172

Music edition ISBN: 0 551 014164

Text set by Barnes Music Engraving Ltd., East Sussex, England
Printed in Great Britain by Hazell Watson and Viney Ltd., Aylesbury, England

Foreword

Mission Praise 1 was originally published as Mission England Praise. Part of the objective of that volume was to meet the growing need of many churches for a supplementary hymn and song book. That objective was extensively fulfilled in thousands of church fellowships throughout the country and, more recently, overseas as well.

In many churches also, however, Mission Praise 1 has become the principle source of music for worship – in spite of its obvious limitations. Those limitations were, principally, the restricted number of items that could be included (only 282) and the almost total exclusion of the many important seasonal items for use at Christmas, Easter, Harvest, etc..

Mission Praise 2 has been specifically compiled to overcome these, and other, limitations. Mission Praise 1 & 2 together now form an all embracing hymn and song book for use throughout the year. They can be used as either a supplement to a traditional hymnbook or, with its large total selection of nearly 650 items, as a complete hymn and song book in its own right.

We have taken advantage of the opportunity also to include many new items which have now passed into widespread popular use during the intervening years. At the same time we have sought to maintain the balance that was achieved in Mission Praise 1 of music from the many different strands and traditions found in today's Christian music.

We pray that, as with Mission Praise 1, this new volume will be extensively used as a means of uniting Christians of all denominations in praise and worship as they work together in the service of the Kingdom of God.

Peter Horrobin and Greg Leavers
June 1987

283
Author unknown
Copyright control

A new commandment I give unto you,
That you love one another as I have loved
you,
That you love one another as I have loved
you.

By this shall all men know that you are my
disciples,
If you have love one for another.
By this shall all men know that you are my
disciples,
If you have love one for another.

284
Martin Luther, 1483–1546
tr. Thomas Carlyle, 1795–1881

1 **A safe stronghold our God is still,**
A trusty shield and weapon;
He'll help us clear from all the ill
That has us now o'ertaken.
The ancient prince of hell
Has ris'n with purpose fell;
Strong mail of craft and pow'r
He weareth in this hour;
On earth is not his fellow.

2 With force of arms we nothing can,
Full soon were we downridden;
But for us fights the proper Man,
Whom God Himself has bidden.
Ask ye: Who is this same?
Christ Jesus is His name,
The Lord Sabaoth's Son;
He, and no other one,
Shall conquer in the battle.

3 And were this world all devils o'er,
And watching to devour us,
We lay it not to heart so sore;
Not they can overpow'r us.
And let the prince of ill
Look grim as e'er he will,
He harms us not a whit:
For why? His doom is writ;
A word shall quickly slay him.

4 God's word, for all their craft and force,
One moment will not linger;
But, spite of hell, shall have its course;
'Tis written by His finger.
And though they take our life,
Goods, honour, children, wife,
Yet is their profit small:
These things shall vanish all;
Th' city of God remaineth.

285
© Timothy Dudley-Smith, b. 1926

1 **Above the voices of the world around
me,**
My hopes and dreams, my cares and loves
and fears,
The long awaited call of Christ has found
me,
The voice of Jesus echoes in my ears:
'I gave my life to break the cords that bind
you,
I rose from death to set your spirit free;
Turn from your sins and put the past behind
you,
Take up your cross and come and follow
me.'

2 What can I offer Him who calls me to Him?
Only the wastes of sin and self and shame;
A mind confused, a heart that never knew
Him,
A tongue unskilled at naming Jesus' Name.
Yet at Your call, and hungry for Your
blessing,
Drawn by that cross which moves a heart of
stone,
Now Lord I come, my tale of sin confessing,
And in repentance turn to You alone.

3 Lord, I believe; help now my unbelieving;
I come in faith because Your promise
stands.
Your word of pardon and of peace
receiving,
All that I am I place within Your hands.
Let me become what You shall choose to
make me,
Freed from the guilt and burden of my sins.
Jesus is mine, who never shall forsake me,
And in His love my new-born life begins.

286
© Kay Chance

1 **Ah Lord God,**
Thou hast made the heavens and the earth
By Thy great power.
Ah Lord God,
Thou hast made the heavens and the earth
By Thine outstretched arm.

2 Nothing is too difficult for Thee,
Nothing is too difficult for Thee.
O great and mighty God,
Great in counsel and mighty in deed,
Nothing, nothing, absolutely nothing,
Nothing is too difficult for Thee.

287

St. Francis of Assisi, 1182–1226
tr. William Henry Draper, 1855–1933

1 **All creatures of our God and King,**
Lift up your voice and with us sing:
Hallelujah, Hallelujah!
Thou burning sun with golden beam,
Thou silver moon with softer gleam:

O praise Him, O praise Him,
Hallelujah, Hallelujah, Hallelujah!

2 Thou rushing wind that art so strong,
Ye clouds that sail in heav'n along,
O praise Him, Hallelujah!
Thou rising morn, in praise rejoice,
Ye lights of evening, find a voice:
O praise Him . . .

3 Thou flowing water, pure and clear,
Make music for thy Lord to hear,
Hallelujah, Hallelujah!
Thou fire so masterful and bright,
That givest man both warmth and light:
O praise Him . . .

4 And all ye men of tender heart,
Forgiving others, take your part,
O sing ye, Hallelujah!
Ye who long pain and sorrow bear,
Praise God and on Him cast your care:
O praise Him . . .

5 Let all things their Creator bless,
And worship Him in humbleness,
O praise Him Hallelujah!
Praise, praise the Father, praise the Son,
And praise the Spirit, Three in One:
O praise Him . . .

288

J. Daniels / P. Thompson
© 1986 Ears & Eyes Music

1 **All earth was dark until You spoke,**
Then all was light and all was peace.
Yet still, oh God, so many wait,
To see the flame of love released.

Lights to the world, oh Light of man,
Kindle in us a mighty flame
Till ev'ry heart, consumed by love,
Shall rise to praise Your holy name.

2 In Christ You gave Your gift of life
To save us from the depth of night.
Oh come and set our spirits free,
And draw us to Your perfect light.
Lights to the world, . . .

3 Where there is fear, may we bring joy,
And healing to a world in pain.
Lord, build Your Kingdom through our lives,
Till Jesus walks this earth again.
Lights to the world, . . .

4 O burn in us that we may burn,
With love that triumphs in despair.
And touch our lives with such a fire,
That souls may search and find You there.
Lights to the world, . . .

289

Theodulph of Orleans, c.750–821
Tr. J.M. Neale, 1818–1866

1 **All glory, laud and honour**
To Thee, Redeemer, King,
To whom the lips of children
Made sweet hosannas ring.
Thou art the King of Israel,
Thou David's royal Son,
Who in the Lord's name comest,
The King and blesséd one.

2 The company of angels
Are praising Thee on high,
And mortal men and all things
Created make reply.
The people of the Hebrews
With psalms before Thee went;
Our praise and prayer and anthems
Before Thee we present.

3 To Thee before Thy passion
They sang their hymns of praise;
To Thee now high exalted
Our melody we raise.
Thou didst accept their praises;
Accept the prayers we bring,
Who in all good delightest,
Thou good and gracious King.

290

Graham Kendrick and Chris Rolinson
© 1986 Thankyou Music

1 **All heaven waits with bated breath,**
For saints on earth to pray.
Majestic angels ready stand
With swords of fiery blade.
Astounding power awaits a word,
From God's resplendent throne
But God awaits our prayer of faith
That cries 'Your will be done.'

2 Awake O church Arise and pray,
Complaining words discard.
The Spirit comes to fill your mouth
With truth, His mighty sword.
Go place your feet on Satan's ground
And there proclaim Christ's name,
In step with heaven's armies march
To conquer and to reign!

3 Now in our hearts and on our lips
The word of faith is near;
Let heaven's will on earth be done, } ladies
Let heaven flow from here.
Come blend your prayers with
Jesus' own
Before the Father's throne; } men
And as the incense clouds ascend
God's holy fire rains down.

4 Soon comes the day when with a shout
King Jesus shall appear,
And with Him all the church
From every age shall fill the air.
The brightness of His coming shall
Consume the lawless one;
As with a word the breath of God
Tears down his rebel throne.

5 One body here by heav'n inspired,
We seek prophetic power.
In Christ agreed one heart and voice
To speak this day and hour.
In every place where chaos rules
And evil forces brood,
Let Jesus voice speak like the roar
Of a great multitude.

291

© 1986 Greg Leavers

**All around me, Lord, I see Your
goodness,**
All creation sings Your praises,
All the world cries, 'God is love!'

292

after J. Neander, 1650–1680
Robert Bridges, 1844–1930

1 **All my hope on God is founded,**
All my trust He shall renew;
He, my guide through changing order,
Only good and only true:
God unknown,
He alone,
Calls my heart to be His own.

2 Pride of man and earthly glory,
Sword and crown betray his trust;
All that human toil can fashion,
Tower and temple, fall to dust;
But God's power
Hour by hour
Is my temple and my tower.

3 Day by day our mighty giver
Grants to us His gifts of love;
In His will our souls find pleasure,
Leading to our home above:
Love shall stand
At His hand,
Joy shall wait for His command.

4 Still from man to God eternal
Sacrifice of praise be done;
High above all praises praising
For the gift of Christ His Son:
Hear Christ's call
One and all –
We who follow shall not fall.

293

Roy Turner
© 1984 Thankyou Music

1 **All over the world the Spirit is moving,**
All over the world as the prophet said it
would be;
All over the world there's a mighty
revelation
Of the glory of the Lord, as the waters cover
the sea.

2 All over His church God's Spirit is moving,
All over His church as the prophet said it
would be;
All over His church there's a mighty
revelation
Of the Glory of the Lord, as the waters
cover the sea.

3 Right here in this place the Spirit is moving,
Right here in this place as the prophet said
it would be;
Right here in this place there's a mighty
revelation
Of the Glory of the Lord, as the waters
cover the sea.

294
Charles Wesley, 1707–88

1 **All praise to our redeeming Lord,**
Who joins us by His grace,
And bids us each to each restored,
Together seek His face.

2 He bids us build each other up;
And, gathered into one,
To our high calling's glorious hope
We hand in hand go on.

3 The gift which He on one bestows,
We all delight to prove;
The grace through every vessel flows,
In purest streams of love.

4 Even now we think and speak the same,
And cordially agree;
Concentrated all, through Jesu's name,
In perfect harmony.

5 We all partake the joy of one,
The common peace we feel,
A peace to sensual minds unknown,
A joy unspeakable.

6 And if our fellowship below
In Jesus be so sweet,
What heights of rapture shall we know
When round His throne we meet.

295
W. Kethe, d. 1594
© in this version Jubilate Hymns

1 **All people that on earth do dwell**
Sing to the Lord with cheerful voice:
Serve Him with joy, His praises tell,
Come now before Him and rejoice!
Know that the Lord is God indeed,
He formed us all without our aid;
We are the flock He loves to feed,
The sheep who by His hand are made.

2 O enter then His gates with praise,
And in His courts His love proclaim;
Give thanks and bless Him all your days:
Let every tongue confess His name.
The Lord our mighty God is good,
His mercy is for ever sure;
His truth at all times firmly stood,
And shall from age to age endure.

3 All people that on earth do dwell
Sing to the Lord with cheerful voice:
Serve Him with joy, His praises tell,
Come now before Him and rejoice!
Praise God the Father, God the Son,
And God the Spirit evermore;
All praise to God the three-in-one,
Let heaven rejoice and earth adore!

296
Fanny J. Crosby, 1820-1915

1 **All the way my Saviour leads me:**
What have I to ask beside?
Can I doubt His tender mercy,
Who through life has been my Guide?
Heav'nly peace, divinest comfort,
Here by faith in Him to dwell!
For I know whate'er befall me,
Jesus doeth all things well.

2 All the way my Saviour leads me:
Cheers each winding path I tread;
Gives me grace for ev'ry trial,
Feeds me with the living bread.
Though my weary steps may falter,
And my soul a-thirst may be,
Gushing from the rock before me,
Lo! a spring of joy I see.

3 All the way my Saviour leads me:
O the fulness of His love!
Perfect rest to me is promised
In my Father's house above.
When my spirit, clothed immortal,
Wings its flight to realms of day,
This, my song through endless ages,
Jesus led me all the way.

297
Andy and Becky Silver
© 1987 Andy Silver

All my life, Lord, to You I want to give;
This is my worship, please show me how to
live.
Take every part of me, make it Your own,
Me on the cross, Lord, You on the throne.

298
Cecil F. Alexander, 1818–95

All things bright and beautiful,
All creatures great and small,
All things wise and wonderful,
The Lord God made them all.

1 Each little flower that opens,
Each little bird that sings,
He made their glowing colours,
He made their tiny wings.
All things bright . . .

2 The purple headed mountain,
The river running by,
The sunset, and the morning
That brightens up the sky;
All things bright . . .

3 The cold wind in the winter,
The pleasant summer sun,
The ripe fruits in the garden,
He made them every one.
All things bright . . .

4 He gave us eyes to see them,
And lips that we might tell
How great is God almighty,
Who has made all things well.
All things bright . . .

299
Austin Martin
© 1983 Thankyou Music

Almighty God, we bring You praise
For Your Son, the Word of God,
By whose power the world was made,
By whose blood we are redeemed.
Morning star, the Father's glory,
We now worship and adore You.
In our hearts Your light has risen;
Jesus, Lord, we worship You.

300
G.W. Conder, 1821–74

1 **All things praise Thee, Lord most high,**
Heaven and earth and sea and sky,
All were for Thy glory made,
That Thy greatness, thus displayed,
Should all worship bring to Thee;
All things praise Thee: Lord, may we.

2 All things praise Thee: night to night
Sings in silent hymns of light;
All things praise Thee: day to day
Chants Thy power in burning ray;
Time and space are praising Thee;
All things praise Thee, Lord, may we.

3 All things praise Thee, high and low,
Rain and dew, and seven-hued bow,
Crimson sunset, fleecy cloud,
Rippling stream, and tempest loud,
Summer, winter – all to Thee
Glory render: Lord, may we.

4 All things praise Thee, heaven's high shrine
Rings with melody divine;
Lowly bending at Thy feet,
Seraph and archangel meet;
This their highest bliss, to be
Ever praising: Lord, may we.

5 All things praise Thee, gracious Lord,
Great Creator, powerful Word,
Omnipresent Spirit, now
At Thy feet we humbly bow,
Lift our hearts in praise to Thee;
All things praise Thee, Lord, may we.

301
Dave Bilbrough
© 1983 Thankyou Music

1 **An army of ordinary people,**
A kingdom where love is the key,
A city, a light to the nations,
Heirs to the promise are we.
A people whose life is in Jesus,
A nation together we stand.
Only through grace are we worthy,
Inheritors of the land.

A new day is dawning,
A new age to come,
When the children of promise
Shall flow together as one:
A truth long neglected,
But the time has now come,
When the children of promise
Shall flow together as one.

2 A people without recognition,
But with Him a destiny sealed,
Called to a heavenly vision:
His purpose shall be fulfilled.
Come let us stand strong together,
Abandon ourselves to the King.
His love shall be ours for ever,
This victory song we shall sing.
A new day . . .

302
J. Montgomery, 1771–1854
© in this version Jubilate Hymns

1 **Angels from the realms of glory,**
Wing your flight through all the earth;
Heralds of creation's story,
Now proclaim Messiah's birth!

Come and worship,
Christ, the new-born King:
Come and worship,
Worship Christ the new-born King.

Shepherds in the fields abiding,
Watching by your flocks at night,
God with man is now residing:
See, there shines the infant light!
Come and worship . . .

Wise men, leave your contemplations!
Brighter visions shine afar;
Seek in Him the hope of nations,
You have seen His rising star:
Come and worship . . .

Though an infant now we view Him,
He will share His Father's throne,
Gather all the nations to Him;
Every knee shall then bow down:
Come and worship . . .

303

© 1983 Martin Nystrom /
Restoration Music Ltd

As the deer pants for the water,
So my soul longs after You.
You alone are my heart's desire
And I long to worship You.

*You alone are my strength, my shield,
To You alone may my spirit yield.
You alone are my heart's desire
And I long to worship You.*

I want You more than gold or silver,
Only You can satisfy.
You alone are the real joy-giver
And the apple of my eye.
You alone are . . .

You're my Friend and You are my Brother,
Even though You are a King.
I love You more than any other,
So much more than anything.
You alone are . . .

304

Francis Pott 1832–1909

Angel voices ever singing
Round thy throne of light,
Angel harps for ever ringing,
Rest not day nor night;
Thousands only live to bless Thee,
And confess Thee Lord of might.

Thou who art beyond the farthest
Mortal eye can scan,
Can it be that Thou regardest
Songs of sinful man?
Can we know that Thou art near us
And wilt hear us? Yes, we can.

3 Yes, we know that Thou rejoicest
O'er each work of Thine;
Thou didst ears and hands and voices
For Thy praise design;
Craftsman's art and music's measure
For Thy pleasure all combine.

4 In Thy house, great God, we offer
Of Thine own to Thee,
And for Thine acceptance proffer,
All unworthily,
Hearts and minds and hands and voices
In our choicest psalmody.

5 Honour, glory, might, and merit
Thine shall ever be,
Father, Son, and Holy Spirit,
Blessèd Trinity.
Of the best that Thou hast given
Earth and heaven render Thee.

305

W.C. Dix, 1837–98
Altered © 1986 Horrobin/Leavers

1 **As with gladness men of old**
Did the guiding star behold;
As with joy they hailed its light,
Leading onward, beaming bright,
So, most gracious God, may we
Led by You for ever be.

2 As with joyful steps they sped,
Saviour, to Your lowly bed,
There to bend the knee before
You whom heaven and earth adore,
So may we with one accord,
Seek forgivness from our Lord.

3 As they offered gifts most rare
Gold and frankincense and myrrh
So may we cleansed from our sin
Lives of service now begin
As in love our treasures bring,
Christ, to You our heavenly King.

4 Holy Jesus, every day
Keep us in the narrow way;
And when earthly things are past,
Bring our ransomed souls at last
Where they need no star to guide,
Where no clouds Your glory hide.

5 In heavenly country bright
Need they no created light
You its light, its joy its crown,
You its sun which goes not down.
There for ever may we sing
Hallelujahs to our King.

306
Henry Twells, 1823–1900

1 **At even, ere the sun was set,**
The sick, O Lord, around Thee lay;
O in what divers pains they met!
O with what joy they went away!

2 Once more 'tis eventide, and we
Oppressed with various ills draw near:
What if Thy form we cannot see?
We know and feel that Thou art here.

3 O Saviour Christ, our woes dispel:
For some are sick; and some are sad;
And some have never loved Thee well;
And some have lost the love they had.

4 And some have found the world is vain,
Yet from the world they break not free;
And some have friends who give them pain,
Yet have not sought a Friend in Thee.

5 And none, O Lord, have perfect rest,
For none are wholly free from sin;
And they who fain would serve thee best
Are concious most of wrong within.

6 O Saviour Christ, Thou too art Man;
Thou hast been troubled, tempted, tried;
Thy kind but searching glance can scan
The very wounds that shame would hide.

7 Thy touch has still its ancient power;
No word from Thee can fruitless fall;
Hear, in this solemn evening hour,
And in Thy mercy heal us all.

307
Janis Miller
© 1983 Christian Fellowship of Columbia

At Your feet, O Lord, we wait for You,
Yearning Lord, hungry Lord, for more of
You.
Bowed before You, Lord, we desire only
You:
Fill us Lord, revive us Lord, with more of
You.

308
Dave Fellingham
© 1982 Thankyou Music

1 **At Your feet we fall, mighty risen Lord,**
As we come before Your throne to worship
You.
By Your Spirit's power You now draw our
hearts,
And we hear Your voice in triumph ringing
clear.

*I am He that liveth, that liveth and was
dead.*
Behold, I am alive for evermore.

2 There we see You stand, mighty risen Lord
Clothed in garments pure and holy, shining
bright.
Eyes of flashing fire, feet like burnished
bronze,
And the sound of many waters is Your
voice.
I am He that liveth . . .

3 Like the shining sun in its noonday strength,
We now see the glory of Your wondrous
face.
Once that face was marred, but now You're
glorified,
And Your words like a two-edged sword
have mighty power.
I am He that liveth . . .

309
David J. Hadden
© 1981 Springtide / Word Music (UK)

Awake, awake, O Zion,
Come clothe yourself with strength.
Awake, awake, O Zion,
Come clothe yourself with strength.

1 Put on your garments of splendour,
O Jerusalem.
Come sing your songs of joy and triumph,
See that your God reigns.
Awake, awake . . .

2 Burst into songs of joy together,
O Jerusalem.
The Lord has comforted His people,
The redeemed Jerusalem.
Awake, awake . . .

310

Away in a manger, no crib for a bed,
The little Lord Jesus laid down His sweet
head.
The stars in the bright sky looked down
where He lay,
The little Lord Jesus asleep in the hay.

The cattle are lowing, the Baby awakes,
But little Lord Jesus, no crying He makes.
I love You Lord Jesus! Look down from the
sky,
And stay by my side until morning is nigh.

Be near me, Lord Jesus; I ask You to stay
Close by me for ever and love me, I pray.
Bless all the dear children in Your tender
care,
And fit us for heaven to live with You there.

11 John Fawcett, 1740–1817, altd.

Blest be the tie that binds
Our hearts in Christian love;
The fellowship of kindred minds
Is like to that above.

Before our Father's throne
We pour our ardent prayers;
Our fears, our hopes, our aims are one,
Our comforts and our cares.

We share our mutual woes,
Our mutual burdens bear,
And often for each other flows
The sympathizing tear.

When for awhile we part,
This thought will soothe our pain,
That we shall still be joined in heart,
And hope to meet again.

This glorious hope revives
Our courage by the way,
While each in expectation lives,
And longs to see the day.

From sorrow, toil, and pain,
And sin we shall be free;
And perfect love and friendship reign
Through all eternity.

312

**Be bold, Be strong, for the Lord your
God is with you,**
Be bold, Be strong, for the Lord your God is
with you,
I am not afraid (No! No! No!)
I am not dismayed,
For I'm walking in faith and victory,
Come on and walk in faith and victory
For the Lord your God is with you.

313 Betty Lou Mills
© 1979 Thankyou Music

Blessed are the pure in heart,
For they shall see God.
Blessed are the pure in heart,
For they shall see God.

1 To see God, the Alpha and Omega,
To see God, Creator life sustainer,
To see God, to think that this is possibility.
Blessed are . . .

2 To see God, the everlasting Father.
To see God, whose love endures for ever.
To see God, how wonderful to think that this
could be.
Blessed are . . .

3 To see God, the God who talked with
Moses.
To see God, whose mercies are so endless.
To see God, what better incentive for
purity.
Blessed are . . .

4 To see God, the One I've loved and longed
for.
To see God, the Father of my Saviour.
To see God, a dream come true, at last His
face I'll see.
Blessed are . . .

314 From Romans 8
© Timothy Dudley-Smith, b. 1926

1 **Born by the Holy Spirit's breath,**
Loosed from the law of sin and death;
Now cleared in Christ from every claim
No judgement stands against our name.

2 In us the Spirit makes His home
That we in Him may overcome;
Christ's risen life, in all its powers,
Its all-prevailing strength, is ours.

3 Sons, then, and heirs of God most high,
We by His Spirit 'Father' cry;
That Spirit with our spirit shares
To frame and breathe our wordless
    prayers.

4 One is His love, His purpose one:
To form the likeness of His Son
In all who, called and justified,
Shall reign in glory at His side.

5 Nor death nor life, nor powers unseen,
Nor height nor depth can come between;
We know through peril, pain and sword,
The love of God in Christ our Lord.

315 Geoffrey Ainger
© 1964 Stainer & Bell Ltd

1 **Born in the night, Mary's child,**
A long way from Your home;
Coming in need, Mary's child,
Born in a borrowed room.

2 Clear shining light, Mary's child,
Your face lights up our way;
Light of the world, Mary's child,
Dawn on our darkened day.

3 Truth of our life, Mary's child,
You tell us God is good;
Prove it is true, Mary's child,
Go to Your cross of wood.

4 Hope of the world Mary's child,
You're coming soon to reign;
King of the earth, Mary's child,
Walk in our streets again.

316 Mary A. Lathbury, 1841–1913
v.2 Alexander Groves, 1843–1909

1 **Break Thou the bread of life, dear Lord
to me,**
As thou didst break the bread beside the
    sea;
Beyond the sacred page I seek Thee, Lord,
My Spirit longs for Thee, Thou living Word.

2 Thou art the bread of life, O Lord, to me,
Thy holy Word the truth that saveth me;
Give me to eat and live with Thee above,
Teach me to love Thy truth, for Thou art
    love.

3 O send Thy Spirit, Lord, now unto me,
That He may touch my eyes and make me
    see;
Show me the truth concealed within Thy
    Word,
And in Thy book revealed, I see Thee,
    Lord.

4 Bless Thou the bread of life to me, to me,
As Thou didst bless the loaves by Galilee;
Then shall all bondage cease, all fetters fall,
And I shall find my peace, my all in all.

317 Reginald Heber, 1783–1826

1 **Brightest and best of the sons of the
    morning,**
Dawn on our darkness and lend us thine
    aid;
Star of the east the horizon adoring,
Guide where our infant Redeemer is laid.

2 Cold on His cradle the dew-drops are
    shining;
Low lies His head with the beasts of the stall;
Angels adore Him, in slumber reclining,
Maker and monarch, and Saviour of all.

3 Say, shall we yield Him, in costly devotion,
Odours of Edom, and offerings divine;
Gems of the mountain, and pearls of the
    ocean,
Myrrh from the forest, or gold from the
    mine?

4 Vainly we offer each ample oblation;
Vainly with gifts would His favour secure;
Richer by far is the heart's adoration;
Dearer to God are the prayers of the poor.

5 Brightest and best of the sons of the
    morning,
Dawn on our darkness and lend us thine
    aid;
Star of the east the horizon adorning,
Guide where our infant Redeemer is laid.

318 Janet Lunt
© 1983 Mustard Seed Music

Broken for me, broken for you,
The Body of Jesus broken for you.

1 He offered His body He poured out His Soul
Jesus was broken that we might be whole:
    Broken for me . . .

Come to My table and with Me dine,
Eat of My bread and drink of My wine:
Broken for me . . .

This is My body given for you,
Eat it rememb'ring I died for you:
Broken for me . . .

This is my blood I shed for you,
For your forgiveness, making you new:
Broken for me . . .

319

R. Edward Miller
© 1974 Maranatha! Music

Cause me to come to Thy river, O Lord,
(three times)
Cause me to come, cause me to drink, cause
me to live.

Cause me to drink from Thy river, O Lord,
(three times)
Cause me to come, cause me to drink, cause
me to live.

Cause me to live by Thy river, O Lord,
(three times)
Cause me to come, cause me to drink, cause
me to live.

320

Charles Wesley, 1707–88

Christ, whose glory fills the skies,
Christ, the true, the only light,
Sun of righteousness, arise,
Triumph o'er the shades of night;
Dayspring from on high, be near;
Daystar, in my heart appear.

Dark and cheerless is the morn
Unaccompanied by Thee;
Joyless is the day's return,
Till Thy mercy's beams I see;
Till they inward light impart,
Glad my eyes, and warm my heart.

Visit then this soul of mine,
Pierce the gloom of sin and grief;
Fill me, radiancy divine,
Scatter all my unbelief;
More and more Thyself display,
Shining to the perfect day.

321

Eddie Espinosa
© 1982 Mercy Music / Thankyou Music

**Change my heart, O God, make it ever
true,**
Change my heart, O God, may I be like
You.

You are the potter, I am the clay,
Mould me and make me, this is what I pray.

Change my heart, O God, make it ever true,
Change my heart, O God, may I be like
You.

322

John Samuel Bewley Monsell, 1811–75

1   **Christ is risen! Hallelujah!**
Risen our victorious Head!
Sing His praises! Hallelujah!
Christ is risen from the dead.
Gratefully our hearts adore Him,
As His light once more appears,
Bowing down in joy before Him,
Rising up from grief and tears.

Christ is risen! Hallelujah!
Risen our victorious Head!
Sing His praises! Hallelujah!
Christ is risen from the dead.

2   Christ is risen! All the sadness
Of His earthly life is o'er,
Through the open gates of gladness
He returns to life once more;
Death and hell before Him bending,
He doth rise, the Victor now,
Angels on His steps attending,
Glory round His wounded brow.
Christ is risen! . . .

3   Christ is risen! Henceforth never
Death or hell shall us enthral,
We are Christ's, in Him for ever
We have triumphed over all;
All the doubting and dejection
Of our trembling hearts have ceased:
'Tis His day of resurrection,
Let us rise and keep the feast.
Christ is risen! . . .

323

Christopher Idle, b. 1938

1 **Christ is surely coming, bringing His
    reward,**
   Omega and Alpha, first and last and Lord:
   Root and stem of David, brilliant morning
       star,
   Meet your Judge and Saviour, nations near
       and far!
   Meet your Judge and Saviour, nations near
       and far!

2 See the holy city! There they enter in,
   Men by Christ made holy, washed from
       every sin:
   Thirsty ones, desiring all He loves to give,
   Come for living water, freely drink, and
       live!
   Come for living water, freely drink, and
       live!

3 Grace be with God's people! Praise His holy
       name!
   Father, Son, and Spirit, evermore the same.
   Hear the certain promise from the eternal
       home:
   'Surely I come quickly!' – Come, Lord Jesus,
       come!
   'Surely I come quickly!' – Come, Lord Jesus,
       come!

324

Charles Wesley, 1707–88

1 **Christ, the Lord, is risen today:**
   Hallelujah!
   Sons of men and angels say,
   Hallelujah!
   Raise your joys and triumphs high;
   Hallelujah!
   Sing, ye heav'ns; thou earth, reply,
   Hallelujah!

2 Love's redeeming work is done;
   Hallelujah!
   Fought the fight, the battle won:
   Hallelujah!
   Lo! our Sun's eclipse is o'er!
   Hallelujah!
   Lo! He sets in blood no more!
   Hallelujah!

3 Vain the stone, the watch, the seal!
   Hallelujah!
   Christ hath burst the gates of hell:
   Hallelujah!
   Death in vain forbids Him rise;
   Hallelujah!
   Christ hath opened paradise.
   Hallelujah!

4 Lives again our glorious King!
   Hallelujah!
   Where, O death, is now thy sting?
   Hallelujah!
   Once He died our souls to save;
   Hallelujah!
   Where thy victory, O grave?
   Hallelujah!

5 Soar we now where Christ hath led,
   Hallelujah!
   Following our exalted Head:
   Hallelujah!
   Made like Him, like Him we rise,
   Hallelujah!
   Ours the cross, the grave, the skies.
   Hallelujah!

6 Hail the Lord of earth and heaven,
   Hallelujah!
   Praise to Thee by both be given;
   Hallelujah!
   Thee we greet, in triumph sing
   Hallelujah!
   Hail, our resurrected King.
   Hallelujah!

325

John Byrom, 1692–1763, altd.

1 **Christians awake! salute the happy
       morn,**
   Whereon the Saviour of mankind was born
   Rise to adore the mystery of love
   Which hosts of angels chanted from above;
   With them the joyful tidings first begun
   Of God incarnate, of the Virgin's Son.

2 Then to the watchful shepherds it was told,
   Who heard the angelic herald's voice
       'Behold,
   I bring good tidings of a Saviour's birth
   To you and all the nations upon earth:
   This day hath God fulfilled His promised
       word,
   This day is born a Saviour, Christ the Lord.

3 He spake; and straightway the celestial
       choir,
   In hymns of joy unknown before conspire;
   High praise of God's redeeming love they
       sang,
   And heaven's whole orb with hallelujahs
       rang:
   God's highest glory was their anthem still,
   'On earth be peace, and unto men
       goodwill.'

O may we keep and ponder in our mind
God's wondrous love in saving lost
    mankind;
Trace we the Babe who hath retrieved our
    loss,
From His poor manger to His bitter cross;
Tread in His steps, assisted by His grace,
Till man's first heavenly state again takes
    place.

Then may we hope, the angelic hosts
    among,
To sing, redeemed, a glad triumphant song:
He that was born upon this joyful day
Around us all His glory shall display;
Saved by His love, incessant we shall sing
Eternal praise to heaven's almighty King.

326
Valerie Collison
© 1972 High-Fye Music Ltd.

Come and join the celebration,
It's a very special day;
Come and share our jubilation,
There's a new King born today!

See the shepherds
Hurry down to Bethlehem;
Gaze in wonder
At the Son of God who lay before them.
    Come and join . . .

Wise men journey,
Led to worship by a star,
Kneel in homage,
Bringing precious gifts from lands afar, So,
    Come and join . . .

'God is with us,'
'Round the world the message bring,
He is with us,
'Welcome', all the bells on earth are
    peeling.
    Come and join . . .

327
Mike Kerry
© 1982 Thankyou Music

Come and praise the living God,
Come and worship, come and worship.
He has made you priest and king,
Come and worship the living God.

1 We come not to a mountain of fire and
    smoke,
   Not to gloom and darkness or trumpet
    sound;
   We come to the new Jerusalem,
   The holy city of God.
    Come and praise . . .

2 By His voice He shakes the earth,
   His judgements known throughout the
    world.
   But we have a city that for ever stands,
   The holy city of God.
    Come and praise . . .

328
© 1985 Andy Silver

Come let us bow down in worship,
Let us kneel before the Lord our Maker.
Come let us bow down in worship,
For He is our God and we are His people,

For He is our God, the people of His
    pasture,
The flock under His care.
Come let us bow down in worship,
Let us kneel before the Lord.

329
after S. Suzanne Toolan
© Michael Baughan
and GIA Publications Incorporated

1 **Come let us worship Christ,**
   To the glory of God the Father,
   For He is worthy of all our love;
   He died and rose for us!
   Praise Him as Lord and Saviour.

    And when the trumpet shall sound,
    And Jesus comes in great power,
    Then He will raise us to be with Him
    For evermore.

2 'I am the bread of life;
   He who comes to Me shall not hunger:
   And all who trust in Me shall not thirst' –
   This is what Jesus said:
   Praise Him as Lord and Saviour.
    And when the trumpet . . .

3 'I am the door to life;
   He who enters by Me is saved,
   Abundant life He will then receive' –
   This is what Jesus said:
   Praise Him as Lord and Saviour.
    And when the trumpet . . .

4 'I am the light of the world;
If you follow Me, darkness ceases,
And in its place comes the light of life; –
This is what Jesus said:
Praise Him as Lord and Saviour,
And when the trumpet . . .

5 Lord, we are one with You;
We rejoice in Your new creation:
Our hearts are fired by Your saving love –
Take up our lives, O Lord,
And use us for Your glory.
And when the trumpet . . .

330
Patricia Morgan
© 1984 Thankyou Music

Come on and celebrate
His gift of love, we will celebrate
The Son of God who loved us
And gave us life.

We'll shout Your praise, O King,
You give us joy nothing else can bring,
We'll give to You our offering
In celebration praise.

Come on and celebrate,
Celebrate, celebrate and sing,
Celebrate and sing to the King.
Come on and celebrate,
Celebrate, celebrate and sing,
Celebrate and sing to the King.

331
Graham Kendrick
© 1985 Thankyou Music

Come see the beauty of the Lord,
Come see the beauty of His face.
See the Lamb that once was slain,
See on His palms is carv'd your name.
See how our pain has pierc'd His heart,
And on His brow He bears our pride;
A crown of thorns.

But only love pours from His heart
As silently He takes the blame.
He has my name upon His lips,
My condemnation falls on Him.
This love is marvellous to me,
His sacrifice has set me free
And now I live.

Come see the beauty of the Lord,
Come see the beauty of His face.

332
J.C. Winslow, 1882–1974
© Mrs J. Tyrell

1 **Come sing the praise of Jesus,**
Sing His love with hearts aflame.
Sing His wondrous birth of Mary
When to save the world He came.
Tell the life He lived for others
And His mighty deeds proclaim,
For Jesus Christ is King.

Praise and glory be to Jesus.
Praise and glory be to Jesus.
Praise and glory be to Jesus,
For Jesus Christ is King.

2 When foes arose and slew Him,
He was victor in the fight;
Over death and hell He triumphed
In His resurrection-might;
He has raised our fallen manhood
And enthroned it in the height,
For Jesus Christ is King.
Praise and glory . . .

3 There's joy for all who serve Him,
More than human tongue can say;
There is pardon for the sinner,
And the night is turned to day;
There is healing for our sorrows,
There is music all the way,
For Jesus Christ is King.
Praise and glory . . .

4 We witness to His beauty,
And we spread His love abroad;
And we cleave the host of darkness,
With the Spirit's piercing sword;
We will lead the souls in prison
To the freedom of the Lord,
For Jesus Christ is King.
Praise and glory . . .

5 To Jesus be the glory,
The dominion, and the praise,
He is Lord of all creation,
He is guide of all our ways;
And the world shall be His empire
In the fulness of the days
For Jesus Christ is King.
Praise and glory . . .

333
H. Alford, 1810–71
© in this version Jubilate Hymns

1 **Come, you thankful people, come,**
   Raise the song of harvest home!
   Fruit and crops are gathered in
   Safe before the storms begin:
   God our maker will provide
   For our needs to be supplied:
   Come, with all His people, come,
   Raise the song of harvest home!

2 All the world is God's own field,
   Harvests for His praise to yield;
   Wheat and weeds together sown
   Here for joy or sorrow grown:
   First the blade and then the ear,
   Then the full corn shall appear—
   Lord of harvest, grant that we
   Wholesome grain and pure may be.

3 For the Lord our God shall come
   And shall bring His harvest home;
   He Himself on that great day,
   Worthless things shall take away,
   Give His angels charge at last
   In the fire the weeds to cast,
   But the fruitful ears to store
   In His care for evermore.

4 Even so, Lord, quickly come—
   Bring Your final harvest home!
   Gather all Your people in
   Free from sorrow, free from sin,
   There together purified,
   Ever thankful at Your side—
   Come, with all Your angels, come,
   Bring that glorious harvest home!

334
Dave Fellingham
© 1983 Thankyou Music

Create in me a clean heart, O God,
And renew a right spirit in me.
Create in me a clean heart, O God,
And renew a right spirit in me.

Wash me, cleanse me, purify me,
Make my heart as white as snow.
Create in me a clean heart, O God,
And renew a right spirit in me.

335
Charles Wesley, 1707–88

1 **Come, Thou long-expected Jesus,**
   Born to set Thy people free;
   From our fears and sins release us;
   Let us find our rest in Thee.

2 Israel's strength and consolation,
   Hope of all the earth Thou art;
   Dear desire of every nation,
   Joy of every longing heart.

3 Born thy people to deliver;
   Born a child, and yet a King;
   Born to reign in us for ever;
   Now Thy gracious kingdom bring.

4 By Thine own eternal Spirit
   Rule in all our hearts alone:
   By Thine all-sufficient merit
   Raise us to Thy glorious throne.

336
G.R. Woodward, 1859–1934

1 **Ding dong! Merrily on high**
   In heav'n the bells are ringing:
   Ding dong! Verily the sky
   Is riv'n with angels singing.

      Gloria, Hosanna in excelsis!
      Gloria, Hosanna in excelsis!

2 E'en so here below, below,
   Let steeple bells be swungen,
   And i-o, i-o, i-o,
   By priest and people sungen.
   Gloria . . .

3 Pray you, dutifully prime
   Your matin chime, ye ringers;
   May you beautifully rime
   Your eve-time song, ye singers.
   Gloria . . .

337
© 1985 Andy Silver

Delight yourself in the Lord,
And He will give you the desires of your
   heart.
Commit your way to the Lord;
Trust in Him and He will make your
   righteousness shine,
Shining like the dawn and like the noon day
   sun.

The righteous will dwell in the land for
   ever,
To share His inheritance.

Delight yourself in the Lord,
And He will give you the desires of your
heart.
Commit your way to the Lord,
Commit your way to the Lord.

338
David Bolton
© 1978 Springtide / Word Music

Delight yourselves in the Lord,
Delight yourselves in the Lord,
For He delights in the praises
Of His own people,
For He delights in the praises
Of His own people.

Let your well spring up within
And overflow to one another,
Let your well spring up within
And overflow to the Lord.

339
Achor
© 1980 Springtide/Word Music(UK)

**Draw near to God and He'll draw near
to you,**
Draw near to God and He'll draw near to
you.
Lift up holy hands to Him and sing of what
He's done,
Open up your hearts to Him and praise Him
for His Son.

340
William Whiting, 1825–78

1 **Eternal Father, strong to save,**
Whose arm hath bound the restless wave,
Who bidd'st the mighty ocean deep
Its own appointed limits keep:
O hear us when we cry to Thee
For those in peril on the sea!

2 O Christ, whose voice the waters heard,
And hushed their raging at Thy word,
Who walkedst on the foaming deep,
And calm amid the storm didst sleep:
O hear us when we cry to Thee
For those in peril on the sea!

3 O Holy Spirit, who didst brood
Upon the waters dark and rude,
And bid their angry tumult cease,
And give, for wild confusion, peace:
O hear us when we cry to Thee
For those in peril on the sea!

4 O Trinity of love and power,
Our brethren shield in danger's hour;
From rock and tempest, fire and foe,
Protect them whersoe'er they go:
Thus evermore shall rise to Thee
Glad hymns of praise from land and sea.

341
Michael Card
© 1981 Whole Armor Publishing (USA)

El-Shaddai, El-Shaddai
(God Almighty, God Almighty)
El-Elyon na Adonai
(God in the highest, Oh Lord)
Age to age You're still the same
by the power of the name.
El-Shaddai, El-Shaddai
(God Almighty, God Almighty)
Erkamka na Adonai
(We will love You, Oh Lord)
We will praise and lift You high, El-Shaddai.

1 Through Your love and through the ram
You saved the son of Abraham.
Through the power of Your hand,
Turned the sea into dry land.
To the outcast on her knees
You were the God who really sees
And by Your might You set Your children
free.
El-Shaddai, El-Shaddai . . .

2 Through the years You made it clear,
That the time of Christ was near.
Though the people couldn't see
What Messiah ought to be.
Though Your word contained the plan
They just could not understand.
Your most awesome work was done
Through the frailty of Your Son.
El-Shaddai, El-Shaddai . . .

342
© 1987 Greg Leavers

Emmanuel, (Emmanuel,)
God with us, (God with us,)
Wonderful (Wonderful)
Counsellor, (Counsellor,)
Prince of Peace – a Saviour is born
To redeem the world and His name is Jesus.
King of kings, (King of kings,)
Lord of Lords (Lord of Lords)
is He.

1 God Himself will give a sign;
A virgin shall bear a son
Who shall be called Emmanuel.
Emmanuel . . .

2 People who now walk in darkness
Soon will see the light of Jesus,
He is the light of the world.
Emmanuel . . .

3 Hear a voice cry in the desert,
Clear a way for the Messiah,
Make straight a highway for God.
Emmanuel . . .

4 Bringing good news; healing heartaches
Preaching freedom; releasing captives,
Giving a mantle of praise.
Emmanuel . . .

343
Dave Fellingham
© 1983 Thankyou Music

Eternal God, we come to You,
We come before Your throne.
We enter by a new and living way,
With confidence we come.
We declare Your faithfulness,
Your promises are true;
We will now draw near to worship You.

O holy God, full of justice,
Wisdom and righteousness,
Faithfulness and love,
Your mighty pow'r and Your majesty
Are now revealed to us
In Jesus who has died for our sin,
Jesus who was raised from the dead,
Jesus now exalted on high.

344
Rick Ridings
© 1977,1980 Scripture in Song /
Thankyou Music

Exalt the Lord our God,
Exalt the Lord our God,
And worship at His footstool,
Worship at His footstool;
Holy is He, holy is He.

345
Graham Kendrick
© 1981 Thankyou Music

1 **Father God, we worship You,**
Make us part of all You do.
As You move among us now
We worship You.

2 Jesus King, we worship You,
Help us listen now to You.
As You move among us now
We worship You.

3 Spirit pure, we worship You,
With Your fire our zeal renew.
As You move among us now
We worship You.

346
Frank Houghton, 1894–1972
© Overseas Missionary Fellowship

1 **Facing a task unfinished,**
That drives us to our knees,
A need that, undiminished,
Rebukes our slothful ease,
We who rejoice to know Thee,
Renew before Thy throne
The solemn pledge we owe Thee,
To go and make Thee known.

2 Where other lords beside Thee
Hold their unhindered sway,
Where forces that defied Thee
Defy Thee still today;
With none to heed their crying
For life, and love, and light,
Unnumbered souls are dying,
And pass into the night.

3 We bear the torch that flaming
Fell from the hands of those
Who gave their lives proclaiming
That Jesus died and rose.
Ours is the same commission,
The same glad message ours,
Fired by the same ambition,
To Thee we yield our powers.

4 O Father who sustained them,
O Spirit who inspired,
Saviour, whose love constrained them
To toil with zeal untired,
From cowardice defend us,
From lethargy awake!
Forth on Thine errands send us
To labour for Thy sake.

347

John Eddison, b. 1916
© Scripture Union

1 **Father, although I cannot see**
The future You have planned,
And though the path is sometimes dark
And hard to understand:
Yet give me faith, through joy and pain,
To trace Your loving hand.

2 When I recall that in the past
Your promises have stood
Through each perplexing circumstance
And every changing mood,
I rest content that all things work
Together for my good.

3 Whatever, then, the future brings
Of good or seeming ill,
I ask for strength to follow You
And grace to trust You still;
And I would look for no reward,
Except to do Your will.

348

Ian Smale
© 1984 Thankyou Music

Father God I wonder how I managed
To exist without the knowledge
Of Your parenthood
And Your loving care.
But now I am Your son,
I am adopted in Your family
And I can never be alone,
'Cause Father God
You're there beside me.

I will sing Your praises,
I will sing Your praises,
I will sing Your praises for evermore.
I will sing Your praises,
I will sing Your praises,
I will sing Your praises for evermore.

349

Rick Ridings
© Scripture in Song /
Thankyou Music

1 **Father make us one,**
Father make us one,
That the world may know Thou hast sent the
Son,
Father make us one.

2 Behold how pleasant and how good it is
For brethren to dwell in unity,
For there the Lord commands the blessing,
Life for evermore.

350

© John Richards
Kyrie
based on the 3-fold, 'Lord, have mercy'

1 **Father God, the Lord, Creator,**
By whose hand we all are fed;
In Your mercy recreate us
At the Breaking of the Bread.

2 Christ our Lord, be present with us,
Risen victorious from the dead!
In Your mercy may we know You
In the Breaking of the Bread.

3 Holy Spirit, God's empowering
By whose Life the Church is led;
In Your mercy, send us strengthened
From the Breaking of the Bread.

4 Father, Son and Holy Spirit
Hear our praises – sung and said.
From our hearts comes our Thanksgiving
For the Breaking of the Bread.

351

© 1985 John Richards

1 **Father, sending Your Anointed**
Son to save, forgive, and heal,
And, through Him, Your Holy Spirit
To make our salvation real;

2 Look upon our ills and trouble
And on those who suffer much.
Send Your church the Spirit's unction
In Christ's Name to heal and touch.

3 Grant forgiveness to the faithful;
Bring to unity their prayer,
Use it for Your work unhindered
Through both sacrament and care.

*4 May the *one/ones* to be anointed
Outwardly with oil this hour,
Know Christ's fullest restoration
Through the Holy Spirit's power.

5 Heal Your church. Anoint and send us
Out into the world to tell
Of Your love and blessings to us;
How, in Christ, 'All will be well.'

* Optional verse for when anointing takes place.

352

Carl Tuttle
© Mercy Music / Thankyou Music

1 **Father, we adore You,**
You've drawn us to this place.
We bow down before You,
Humbly on our face.

All the earth shall worship
At the throne of the King.
Of His great and awesome power,
We shall sing!

2 Jesus we love You,
Because You first loved us,
You reached out and healed us
With Your mighty touch.
All the earth . . .

3 Spirit we need You,
To lift us from this mire,
Consume and empower us
With Your holy fire.
All the earth . . .

Holy is He; Blesséd is He;
Worthy is He; Gracious is He;
Faithful is He; Awesome is He;
Saviour is He; Master is He;
Mighty is He.
Have mercy on me.

353

from Psalm 147
© Timothy Dudley-Smith, b. 1926

1 **Fill your hearts with joy and gladness,**
Sing and praise your God and mine!
Great the Lord in love and wisdom,
Might and majesty divine!
He who framed the starry heavens
Knows and names them as they shine.

2 Praise the Lord, His people, praise Him!
Wounded souls His comfort know;
Those who fear Him find His mercies,
Peace for pain and joy for woe;
Humble hearts are high exalted,
Human pride and power laid low.

3 Praise the Lord for times and seasons,
Cloud and sunshine, wind and rain;
Spring to melt the snows of winter
Till the waters flow again;
Grass upon the mountain pasture,
Golden valleys thick with grain.

4 Fill your hearts with joy and gladness,
Peace and plenty crown your days;
Love His laws, declare His judgements,
Walk in all His words and ways;
He the Lord and we His children –
Praise the Lord, all people, praise!

354

Everett Perry
© 1983 Thankyou Music

Father Your love is precious beyond all
loves,
Father Your love overwhelms me.
So I lift up my hands,
An expression of my love,

And I give You my heart
In joyful obedience.
Father Your love is precious beyond all
loves,
Father Your love overwhelms me.

355

Chris A. Bowater
© 1983 Word Music (UK)

Fill the place Lord with Your glory
At this gath'ring of Your own;
Reign in sovereign grace and power
From your praise surrounded throne.

Fill the place Lord with Your glory
At this gath'ring of Your own;
We exalt You, we adore You,
Thankful hearts now join as one.

You're the Christ, the King of glory,
Father's well beloved Son.
Fill the place Lord with Your glory
At this gath'ring of Your own.

356

Folliott Pierpoint, 1835–1917
Altered © 1986 Horrobin/Leavers

1 **For the beauty of the earth,**
For the beauty of the skies,
For the love which from our birth
Over and around us lies,
Father unto You we raise
This our sacrifice of praise.

2 For the beauty of each hour
Of the day and of the night,
Hill and vale and tree and flower,
Sun and moon and stars of light,
Father, unto You we raise
This our sacrifice of praise.

3 For the joy of love from God,
That we share on earth below.
For our friends and family
And the love that they can show,
Father, unto You we raise
This our sacrifice of praise.

4 For each perfect gift divine
To our race so freely given,
Thank You Lord that they are mine,
Here on earth as gifts from heaven.
Father, unto You we raise
This our sacrifice of praise.

357
Dale Garratt
© 1972 Scripture in Song / Thankyou Music

For His name is exalted,
His glory above heaven and earth.
Holy is the Lord God Almighty,
Who was and who is and who is to come.

For His name is exalted,
His glory above heaven and earth.
Holy is the Lord God Almighty,
Who sitteth on the throne and who lives for
evermore.

358
Graham Kendrick
© 1985 Thankyou Music

1 **For this purpose Christ was revealed**
To destroy all the works
Of the Evil One.
Christ in us has overcome,
So with gladness we sing
And welcome His kingdom in.

MEN
Over sin He has conquered,
LADIES
Hallelujah, He has conquered.
MEN
Over death victorious,
LADIES
Hallelujah, victorious.
MEN
Over sickness He has triumphed.
LADIES
Hallelujah, He has triumphed.
ALL
Jesus reigns over all!

2 In the name of Jesus we stand,
By the power of His blood
We now claim this ground.
Satan has no authority here,
Powers of darkness must flee,
For Christ has the victory.
Over sin . . .

359

For unto us a child is born,
Unto us a Son is given;
And the government
Shall be upon His shoulders.

And His name shall be called
Wonderful, Counsellor,
The Mighty God,
The everlasting Father,
And the Prince of Peace is He.

360
G.H. Smyttan, 1822–70, altd.

1 **Forty days and forty nights**
Thou wast fasting in the wild;
Forty days and forty nights
Tempted and yet undefiled.

2 Sunbeams scorching all the day,
Chilly dew-drops nightly shed,
Prowling beasts about Thy way,
Stones Thy pillow, earth Thy bed.

3 Let us Thy endurance share
And from earthly greed abstain,
With Thee watching unto prayer
With Thee strong to suffer pain.

4 Then if evil on us press,
Flesh or spirit to assail,
Victor in the wilderness,
May we never faint or fail!

5 So shall peace divine be ours;
Holier gladness ours shall be;
Come to us angelic powers,
Such as ministered to Thee.

361
Graham Kendrick
© 1983 Thankyou Music

From heav'n You came, helpless babe,
Enter'd our world, Your glory veil'd;
Not to be served but to serve,
And give Your life that we might live.

This is our God, the Servant King,
He calls us now to follow Him,
To bring our lives as a daily offering
Of worship to the Servant King.

There in the garden of tears,
My heavy load He chose to bear;
His heart with sorrow was torn,
'Yet not my will but Yours,' He said.
This is our God . . .

Come see His hands and His feet,
The scars that speak of sacrifice,
Hands that flung stars into space
To cruel nails surrendered.
This is our God . . .

So let us learn how to serve,
And in our lives enthrone Him;
Each other's needs to prefer,
For it is Christ we're serving.
This is our God . . .

362
Charles Wesley, 1707–88

Give me the faith which can remove,
And sink the mountain to a plain.
Give me the childlike, praying love,
Which longs to build Thy house again;
Thy love let it my heart o'erpower,
Let it my ransomed soul devour.

I would the precious time redeem,
And longer live for this alone—
To spend and to be spent for them
Who have not yet my Saviour known;
Fully on these my mission prove,
And only breathe to breathe Thy love.

My talents, gifts, and graces, Lord,
Into Thy blessèd hands receive;
And let me live to preach Thy word,
And let me to Thy glory live;
My every sacred moment spend
In publishing the sinners' friend.

Enlarge, inflame, and fill my heart
With boundless charity divine;
So shall I all my strength exert,
And love them with a zeal like Thine;
And lead them to Thine open side,
The sheep for whom their shepherd died.

363
Isaac Watts, 1674–1748, altd.

1   **Give to our God immortal praise;**
Mercy and truth are all His ways:
Wonders of grace to God belong,
Repeat His mercies in your song.

2   Give to the Lord of lords renown;
The King of kings with glory crown:
His mercies ever shall endure,
When lords and kings are known no more.

3   He built the earth, He spread the sky,
And fixed the starry lights on high:
Wonders of grace to God belong,
Repeat His mercies in your song.

4   He fills the sun with morning light,
He bids the moon direct the night:
His mercies ever shall endure,
When suns and moons shall shine no more.

5   He sent His Son with power to save
From guilt and darkness and the grave:
Wonders of grace to God belong,
Repeat His mercies in your song.

364
© 1984 John Richards / Renewal Servicing
Gloria (based on the 'Gloria' of the
Eucharistic Liturgy)

1   **Glory be to God in Heaven,**
And to all on earth, His Peace.
Lord and Father, King in glory,
Gifts of praise in us release
So our worship and thanksgiving
From our hearts will never cease.

2   Christ incarnate, sent by Father
To redeem, renew, restore;
Risen Lamb, in glory seated,
Hear our prayers, Lord, we implore.
Now to Father, Son and Spirit
Be all glory evermore.

365
© 1986 Greg Leavers

Glory to God in the highest,
Peace upon earth.
Jesus Christ has come to earth,
That's why we sing,
Jesus the King,
Jesus has come for you.

1   The shepherds who were sitting there
Were suddenly filled with fear,
The dark night was filled with light
Angels singing everywhere.
Glory to God . . .

2 The next time we hear a song
Of worship from a heavenly throng,
Will be when Jesus comes again,
Then with triumph we'll all sing,
Glory to God . . .

3 Israel comes to greet the Saviour,
Judah is glad to see His day;
From east and west the peoples travel,
He will show the way.
God has spoken . . .

366
T. Ken, 1637–1710
© in this version Jubilate Hymns

1 **Glory to You, my God, this night**
For all the blessings of the light;
Keep me, O keep me, King of kings,
Beneath Your own almighty wings.

2 Forgive me, Lord, through Your dear Son,
The wrong that I this day have done,
That peace with God and man may be,
Before I sleep, restored to me.

3 Teach me to live, that I may dread
The grave as little as my bed;
Teach me to die, that so I may
Rise glorious at the awesome day.

4 O may my soul on you repose
And restful sleep my eyelids close;
Sleep that shall me more vigorous make
To serve my God when I awake.

5 If in the night I sleepless lie,
My mind with peaceful thoughts supply;
Let no dark dreams disturb my rest,
No powers of evil me molest.

6 Praise God from whom all blessing flow
In heaven above and earth below;
One God, three persons, we adore,
To Him be praise for evermore!

367
© 1966, 1986 Willard F. Jabusch
University of St. Mark of the Lake, Mundelein, Ill.

God has spoken to His people, alleluia,
And His words are words of wisdom,
alleluia!

1 Open your ears, O Christian people,
Open your ears and hear good news;
Open your hearts, O royal priesthood,
God has come to you.
God has spoken . . .

2 They who have ears to hear His message,
They who have ears, then let them hear;
They who would learn the way of wisdom,
Let them hear God's word.
God has spoken . . .

368
Joseph Parker, 1830–1902

1 **God holds the key of all unknown,**
And I am glad:
If other hands should hold the key,
Or if He trusted it to me,
I might be sad, I might be sad.

2 What if tomorrow's cares were here
Without its rest?
I'd rather He unlocked the day,
And, as the hours swing open, say,
'My will is best, My will is best.''

3 The very dimness of my sight
Makes me secure;
For, groping in my misty way,
I feel His hand; I hear Him say,
'My help is sure, My help is sure.'

4 I cannot read His future plans;
But this I know:
I have the smiling of His face,
And all the refuge of His grace,
While here below, while here below.

5 Enough: this covers all my wants;
And so I rest!
For what I cannot, He can see,
And in His care I saved shall be,
For ever blest, for ever blest.

369
© Copyright control

1 **God is building a house,**
God is building a house,
God is building a house that will stand.
He is building by His plan
With the living stones of man,
God is building a house that will stand.

2 God is building a house,
God is building a house,
God is building a house that will stand.
With apostles, prophets, pastors,
With evangelists and teachers,
God is building a house that will stand.

3 Christ is head of this house,
Christ is head of this house,
Christ is head of this house that will stand.
He abideth in its praise,
Will perfect it in its ways,
Christ is head of this house that will stand.

4 We are part of this house,
We are part of this house,
We are part of this house that will stand.
We are called from every nation
To enjoy his full salvation,
We are part of this house that will stand.

370 Graham Kendrick
© 1985 Thankyou Music

God is good, we sing and shout it,
God is good, we celebrate.
God is good, no more we doubt it,
God is good, we know it's true.

And when I think of His love for me,
My heart fills with praise and I feel like
        dancing.
For in His heart there is room for me
And I run with arms open'd wide.

God is good, we sing and shout it,
God is good, we celebrate.
God is good, no more we doubt it,
God is good, we know it's true. *Hey!*

371 Timothy Rees, 1874–1939, altd.
© A.R. Mowbray & Co. Ltd. Oxford

1 **God is love: let heaven adore Him;**
God is love: let earth rejoice;
Let creation sing before Him,
And exalt Him with one voice.
He who laid the earth's foundation,
He who spread the heavens above,
He who breathes through all creation,
He is love, eternal love.

2 God is love: and He enfoldeth
All the world in one embrace;
With unfailing grasp He holdeth
Every child of every race.
And when human hearts are breaking
Under sorrow's iron rod,
All the sorrow, all the aching,
Wrings with pain the heart of God.

3 God is love: and though with blindness
Sin afflicts the souls of men,
God's eternal loving-kindness
Holds and guides them even then.
Sin and death and hell shall never
O'er us final triumph gain;
God is love, so love for ever
O'er the universe must reign.

372 © Richard Bewes, b. 1934

1 **God is our strength and refuge,**
Our present help in trouble;
And we therefore will not fear,
Though the earth should change!
Though mountains shake and tremble,
Though swirling floods are raging,
God the Lord of hosts is with us evermore!

2 There is a flowing river,
Within God's holy city;
God is in the midst of her –
She shall not be moved!
God's help is swiftly given,
Thrones vanish at His presence –
God the Lord of hosts is with us evermore!

3 Come, see the works of our maker,
Learn of His deeds all-powerful;
Wars will cease across the world
When He shatters the spear!
Be still and know your creator,
Uplift Him in the nations –
God the Lord of hosts is with us evermore!

373 A. Ainger, 1841–1919
© in this version Jubilate Hymns

1 **God is working His purpose out,**
As year succeeds to year:
God is working His purpose out,
And the time is drawing near:
Nearer and nearer draws the time,
The time that shall surely be,
When the earth shall be filled
With the glory of God,
As the waters cover the sea.

2 From the utmost east to utmost west
Wherever man has trod,
By the mouth of many messengers
Rings out the voice of God:
Listen to me you continents,
You islands look to me,
That the earth may be filled
With the glory of God,
As the waters cover the sea.

3 We shall march in the strength of God,
  With the banner of Christ unfurled,
  The the light of the glorious gospel of truth
  May shine throughout the world;
  We shall fight with sorrow and sin
  To set their captives free,
  That the earth may be filled
  With the glory of God,
  As the waters cover the sea.

4 All we can do is nothing worth
  Unless God blesses the deed;
  Vainly we hope for the harvest tide
  Till God gives life to the seed:
  Nearer and nearer draws the time,
  The time that shall surely be,
  When the earth shall be filled
  With the glory of God,
  As the waters cover the sea.

374

1 **God save our gracious Queen,**
  Long live our noble Queen,
  God save the Queen!
  Send her victorious,
  Happy and glorious,
  Long to reign over us;
  God save the Queen!

2 Thy choicest gifts in store
  On her be pleased to pour,
  Long may she reign;
  May she defend our laws,
  And ever give us cause
  To sing with heart and voice
  God save the Queen!

375 William Cowper, 1731–1800

1 **God moves in a mysterious way**
  His wonders to perform;
  He plants His footsteps in the sea,
  And rides upon the storm.

2 Deep in unfathomable mines
  Of never-failing skill,
  He treasures up His bright designs,
  And works His sov'reign will.

3 Ye fearful saints, fresh courage take,
  The clouds ye so much dread
  Are big with mercy, and shall break
  In blessings on your head.

4 Judge not the Lord by feeble sense,
  But trust Him for His grace;
  Behind a frowning providence
  He hides a smiling face.

5 His purposes will ripen fast,
  Unfolding every hour;
  The bud may have a bitter taste,
  But sweet will be the flower.

6 Blind unbelief is sure to err,
  And scan His work in vain;
  God is His own interpreter,
  And He will make it plain.

376 Dave Fellingham
© 1982 Thankyou Music

God of glory, we exalt Your name,
You who reign in majesty.
We lift our hearts to You
And we will worship, praise
And magnify Your holy name.

In power resplendent
You reign in glory,
Eternal King,
You reign for ever.

Your word is mighty,
Releasing captives,
Your love is gracious,
You are my God.

377 Christopher Wordsworth, 1807–85

1 **Gracious Spirit, Holy Ghost,**
  Taught by You, we covet most,
  Of Your gifts at Pentecost,
  Holy heavenly love.

2 Faith that mountains could remove,
  Tongues of earth or heaven above,
  Knowledge, all things, empty prove
  Without heavenly love.

3 Though I as a martyr bleed,
  Give my goods the poor to feed,
  All is vain if love I need;
  Therefore give me love.

4 Love is kind, and suffers long,
  Love is meek, and thinks no wrong,
  Love than death itself more strong:
  Therefore give us love.

5 Prophecy will fade away
  Melting in the light of day;
  Love will ever with us stay:
  Therefore give us love.

6 Faith, and hope, and love we see
  Joining hand in hand, agree;
  But the greatest of the three,
  And the best, is love.

378 H.E. Fosdick, 1878–1969

1 **God of grace and God of glory,**
  On Thy people pour Thy power;
  Crown Thine ancient Church's story;
  Bring her bud to glorious flower.
  Grant us wisdom,
  Grant us courage,
  For the facing of this hour.

2 Lo! the hosts of evil round us
  Scorn Thy Christ, assail His ways!
  Fears and doubts too long have bound us;
  Free our hearts to work and praise.
  Grant us wisdom,
  Grant us courage,
  For the living of these days.

3 Heal Thy children's warring madness;
  Bend our pride to Thy control;
  Shame our wanton, selfish gladness,
  Rich in things and poor in soul.
  Grant us wisdom,
  Grant us courage,
  Lest we miss Thy kingdom's goal.

4 Set our feet on lofty places;
  Gird our lives that they may be
  Armoured with all Christlike graces
  In the fight to set men free.
  Grant us wisdom,
  Grant us courage,
  That we fail not man nor Thee.

5 Save us from weak resignation
  To the evils we deplore;
  Let the search for Thy salvation
  Be our glory evermore.
  Grant us wisdom,
  Grant us courage,
  Serving Thee whom we adore.

379 John Mason Neale, 1818–66

1 **Good Christian men, rejoice**
  With heart and soul and voice!
  Give ye heed to what we say:
  News! News! Jesus Christ is born today.
  Ox and ass before Him bow,
  And He is in the manger now:
  Christ is born today,
  Christ is born today.

2 Good Christian men, rejoice
  With heart and soul and voice!
  Now ye hear of endless bliss:
  Joy! Joy! Jesus Christ was born for this.
  He hath oped the heav'nly door,
  And man is blest for evermore.
  Christ was born for this,
  Christ was born for this.

3 Good Christian men, rejoice
  With heart and soul and voice!
  Now ye need not fear the grave:
  Peace! Peace! Jesus Christ was born to save;
  Calls you one, and calls you all,
  To gain His everlasting hall.
  Christ was born to save,
  Christ was born to save.

380 © 1986 Peter Horobin

1 **God whose Son was once a man on
    earth**
  Gave His life that men may live.
  Risen, our ascended Lord
  Fulfilled His promised word.

  When the Spirit came, the church was born,
  God's people shared in a bright new dawn.
  They healed the sick,
  They taught God's word,
  They sought the lost,
  They obeyed the Lord.
  And it's all because the Spirit came
  That the world will never be the same,
  Because the Spirit came.

2 God whose power fell on the early church,
  Sent to earth from heav'n above.
  Spirit led, by Him ordained
  They showed the world God's love.

When the Spirit came, the church was born,
God's people shared in a bright new dawn.
They healed the sick,
They taught God's word,
They sought the lost,
They obeyed the Lord.
And it's all because the Spirit came
That the world will never be the same,
Because the Spirit came.

3 Pour Your Spirit on the church today,
That Your life through me may flow.
Spirit filled, I'll serve Your Name
And live the truth I know.

When the Spirit comes, new life is born,
God's people share in a bright new dawn.
We'll heal the sick,
We'll teach God's word,
We'll seek the lost,
We'll obey the Lord.
And it's all because the Spirit came
That the world will never be the same,
Because the Spirit came.

381   William Cowper, 1731–1800

1 **Hark, my soul! it is the Lord;**
'Tis thy Saviour, hear His word;
Jesus speaks, and speaks to thee,
'Say, poor sinner, lov'st thou Me?'

2 'I delivered thee when bound,
And, when bleeding, healed thy wound;
Sought thee wand'ring, set thee right,
Turned thy darkness into light.'

3 'Mine is an unchanging love,
Higher than the heights above,
Deeper than the depths beneath,
Free and faithful, strong as death.'

4 'Thou shalt see My glory soon,
When the work of grace is done;
Partner of My throne shalt be;
Say, poor sinner, lov'st thou Me?'

5 Lord! it is my chief complaint
That my love is weak and faint;
Yet I love Thee, and adore:
O for grace to love Thee more!

382   C. Wesley, 1707–88 and T. Cotterill, 1779–1823

1 **Hail the day that sees Him rise,** *Alleluia,*
To His throne beyond the skies, *Alleluia,*
Christ, the Lamb for sinners given, *Alleluia,*
Enters now the highest heaven: *Alleluia.*

2 There for Him high triumph waits: *Alleluia,*
Lift your heads, eternal gates, *Alleluia,*
He has conquered death and sin, *Alleluia,*
Take the King of glory in: *Alleluia.*

3 See! the heaven its Lord receives, *Alleluia,*
Yet He loves the earth He leaves; *Alleluia,*
Though returning to His throne, *Alleluia,*
Still He calls mankind His own. *Alleluia.*

4 Still for us He intercedes, *Alleluia,*
His prevailing death He pleads, *Alleluia,*
Near Himself prepares our place, *Alleluia,*
He the first-fruits of our race. *Alleluia.*

5 Lord, though parted from our sight *Alleluia,*
Far beyond the starry height, *Alleluia,*
Lift our hearts that we may rise *Alleluia,*
One with You beyond the skies: *Alleluia.*

6 There with You we shall remain, *Alleluia,*
Share the glory of Your reign, *Alleluia,*
There Your face unclouded view, *Alleluia,*
Find our heaven of heavens in You: *Alleluia.*

383   John Bakewell, 1721–1819

1 **Hail, thou once despisèd Jesus,**
Hail, Thou Galilean King!
Thou didst suffer to release us,
Thou didst free salvation bring.
Hail, Thou agonising Saviour,
Bearer of our sin and shame,
By Thy merits we find favour;
Life is given through Thy Name.

2 Paschal Lamb, by God appointed,
All our sins on Thee were laid.
By Almighty love anointed,
Thou hast full atonement made.
All Thy people are forgiven
Through the virtue of Thy blood:
Opened is the gate of heaven,
Peace is made 'twixt man and God.

3 Jesus, hail! enthroned in glory,
There for ever to abide;
All the heavenly hosts adore Thee,
Seated at Thy Father's side:
There for sinners Thou art pleading,
There Thou dost our place prepare,
Ever for us interceding,
Till in glory we appear.

4 Worship, honour, power, and blessing,
Thou art worthy to receive:
Loudest praises, without ceasing,
Meet it is for us to give:
Help, ye bright angelic spirits,
Bring your sweetest, noblest lays;
Help to sing our Saviour's merits,
Help to chant Immanuel's praise.

384
Charles Wesley, 1707–88
George Whitfield, 1714–70
Martin Madan, 1726–90 and others

1 **Hark! The herald angels sing,**
'Glory to the new-born King!
Peace on earth, and mercy mild,
God and sinners reconciled.'
Joyful, all you nations, rise,
Join the triumph of the skies;
With the angelic host proclaim:
'Christ is born in Bethlehem!'
  Hark! The herald-angels sing,
  'Glory to the new-born King!'

2 Christ by highest heaven adored,
Christ, the everlasting Lord,
Late in time behold Him come,
Offspring of a virgin's womb!
Veiled in flesh the Godhead see!
Hail, the incarnate Deity!
Pleased as man with man to dwell,
Jesus, our Immanuel.
  Hark! The herald-angels sing,
  'Glory to the new-born King!'

3 Hail, the heaven-born Prince of Peace!
Hail, the Sun of Righteousness!
Light and life to all He brings,
Risen with healing in His wings.
Mild He lays His glory by,
Born that man no more may die;
Born to raise the sons of earth,
Born to give them second birth.
  Hark! The herald-angels sing,
  'Glory to the new-born King!'

385
Philip Dodderidge, 1702–1751
Altered © 1986 Horrobin/Leavers

1 **Hark, the glad sound! The Saviour
comes,**
The Saviour promised long;
Let every heart prepare a throne,
And every voice a song.

2 He comes, the prisoners to release
In Satan's bondage held;
The chains of sin before Him break,
The iron fetters yield.

3 He comes to free the captive mind
Where evil thoughts control;
And for the darkness of the blind
Gives light that makes them whole.

4 He comes the broken heart to bind,
The wounded soul to cure;
And with the treasures of His grace
To enrich the humble poor.

5 Our glad hosannas, Prince of Peace,
Your welcome shall proclaim;
And heaven's eternal arches ring
With Your belovéd name.

386 A.A. Pollard, 1862–1934

1 **Have Thine own way, Lord,**
  have Thine own way;
Thou art the potter, I am the clay.
Mould me and make me after thy will,
While I am waiting yielded and still.

2 Have Thine own way, Lord,
  have Thine own way;
Search me and try me, Master, today.
Whiter than snow, Lord, wash me just now,
As in Thy presence humbly I bow.

3 Have Thine own way, Lord,
  have Thine own way;
Wounded and weary, help me, I pray.
Power, all power, surely is Thine;
Touch me and heal me, Saviour Divine.

4 Have Thine own way, Lord,
  have Thine own way;
Hold o'er my being absolute sway.
Fill with Thy Spirit till all shall see
Christ only, always, living in me.

387 © C. Porteous, b. 1935
and in this version Jubilate Hymns

1 **He gave His life in selfless love**
For sinful man He came;
He had no stain of sin Himself
But bore our guilt and shame:
He took the cup of pain and death,
His blood was freely shed;
We see His Body on the cross,
We share the living bread.

2 He did not come to call the good
But sinners to repent;
it was the lame, the deaf, the blind
For whom His life was spent:
To heal the sick, to find the lost –
It was for such He came,
And round His table all may come
To praise His holy name.

3 They heard Him call His Father's name –
Then 'Finished!' was His cry;
Like them we have forsaken Him
And left Him there to die:
The sins that crucified Him then
Are sins His blood was cured;
The love that bound Him to a cross
Our freedom has ensured.

4 His body broken once for us
Is glorious now above;
The cup of blessing we receive,
A sharing of His love:
As in His presence we partake,
His dying we proclaim
Until the hour of majesty
When Jesus comes again.

388 Graham Kendrick
© 1986 Thankyou Music

He that is in us is greater
than he that is in the world.
He that is in us is greater
than he that is in the world.

1 Therefore I will sing and I will rejoice
For His Spirit lives in me.
Christ the living One has overcome
And we share in His victory.
He that is in us . . .

2 All the powers of death and hell and sin
Lie crushed beneath His feet.
Jesus owns the Name above all names
Crowned with honour and majesty.
He that is in us . . .

Repeat verse 2 slowly and majestically.

389 P. Dearmer, 1867–1936
after J. Bunyan, 1628–1688

1 **He who would valiant be**
'Gainst all disaster,
Let him in constancy
Follow the Master.
There's no discouragement
Shall make him once relent,
His first avowed intent
To be a pilgrim.

2 Who so beset him round
With dismal stories,
Do but themselves confound—
His strength the more is.
No foes shall stay his might,
Though he with giants fight:
He will make good his right
To be a pilgrim.

3 Since, Lord, You do defend
Us with Your Spirit,
We know we at the end
Shall life inherit.
Then fancies flee away!
I'll fear not what men say,
I'll labour night and day
To be a pilgrim.

390 © Marshall, Morgan and Scott

1 **He's got the whole wide world in His**
hands,
He's got the whole wide world in His hands,
He's got the whole wide world in His hands,
He's got the whole world in His hands.

2 He's got ev'rybody here, in His hands,
He's got ev'rybody here, in His hands,
He's got ev'rybody here, in His hands,
He's got the whole world in His hands.

3 He's got the tiny little baby, in His hands,
He's got the tiny little baby, in His hands,
He's got the tiny little baby, in His hands,
He's got the whole world in His hands.

4 He's got you and me brother, in His hands,
He's got you and me brother, in His hands,
He's got you and me brother, in His hands,
He's got the whole world in His hands.

391

1 **Healing God, Almighty Father,**
Active throughout history;
Ever saving, guiding, working
For Your children to be free.
Shepherd, King, inspiring prophets
To foresee Your suffering role –
Lord, we raise our prayers and voices
Make us one and make us whole.

2 Healing Christ, God's Word incarnate,
Reconciling man to man.
God's atonement, dying for us
In His great redemptive plan.
'Jesus', Saviour, Healer, Victor
Drawing out for us death's sting,
Lord, we bow our hearts in worship,
And united praises bring.

3 Healing Spirit, Christ-annointing
Raising to new Life in Him;
Help the poor; release to captives;
Cure of body; health within.
Life-renewing and empowering
Christ-like service to the lost.
Lord, we pray 'Renew Your wonders
As of a New Pentecost!'

4 Healing Church, called-out and chosen
To enlarge God's Kingdom here.
Lord-obeying; Spirit-strengthened
To bring God's salvation near.
For creation's reconciling
Gifts of love in us release.
Father, Son and Holy Spirit
'Make us instruments of peace.'

392

Hear my cry, O God,
Listen to my prayer;
From the ends of the earth
Will I call to you.
Hear my cry, O God,
When my heart is overwhelmed;
Lead me to the rock
That is higher than I.

Teach me to trust in You,
To pour out my heart to You;
You're my help,
My refuge and my strength.
Hear my cry, O God,
Listen to my prayer;
From the ends of the earth
Will I call to you.
Hear my cry, O God.

393

Here I am, wholly available.
As for me, I will serve the Lord.

1 The fields are white unto harvest
But O, the lab'rers are so few,
So Lord I give myself to help the reaping,
To gather precious souls unto You.
Here I am . . .

2 The time is right in the nation
For works of power and authority;
God's looking for a people who are willing
To be counted in His glorious victory.
Here I am . . .

3 As salt are we ready to savour,
In darkness are we ready to be light,
God's seeking out a very special people
To manifest His truth and His might.
Here I am . . .

394

1 **Here, O my Lord, I see Thee face to face;**
Here would I touch and handle things unseen,
Here grasp with firmer hand th'eternal grace,
And all my weariness upon Thee lean.

2 Here would I feed upon the bread of God,
Here drink with Thee the royal wine of heav'n;
Here would I lay aside each earthly load,
Here taste afresh the calms of sin forgiv'n.

3 Too soon we rise, the symbols disappear;
The feast, though not the love, as past and gone;
The bread and wine remove, but Thou art here,
Nearer than ever, still my Shield and Sun.

4 I have no help but Thine; nor do I need
Another arm save Thine to lean upon;
It is enough, my Lord, enough indeed;
My strength is in Thy might, Thy might alone.

5 Mine is the sin, but Thine the righteousness;
Mine is the guilt, but Thine the cleansing blood;
Here is my robe, my refuge, and my peace—
Thy blood, Thy righteousness, O Lord my God.

6 Feast after feast thus comes and passes by,
Yet, passing, points to the glad feast above,
Giving sweet foretaste of the festal joy,
The Lamb's great bridal feast of bliss and
love.

395 Robert Whitney Manzano
© 1984 Thankyou Music

He gave me beauty for ashes,
The oil of joy for mourning,
The garment of praise
For the spirit of heaviness.
That we might be trees of righteousness,
The planting of the Lord,
That He might be glorified.

396 Chorus Traditional Israeli song
Verses © Michael Baughen

Hévénu shalom aléchem,
Hévénu shalom aléchem,
Hévénu shalom aléchem,
Hévénu shalom, shalom, shalom aléchem.

1 Because He died and is risen,
Because He died and is risen,
Because He died and is risen,
We now have peace with God
        through Jesus Christ our Lord.
        Hévénu shalom . . .

2 His peace destroys walls between us,
His peace destroys walls between us,
His peace destroys walls between us,
For only He can reconcile
        us both to God.
        Hévénu shalom . . .

3 My peace I give you, said Jesus,
My peace I give you, said Jesus,
My peace I give you, said Jesus,
Don't let your heart be troubled,
        do not be afraid.
        Hévénu shalom . . .

4 The peace beyond understanding,
The peace beyond understanding,
The peace beyond understanding,
Will guard the hearts and minds
        of those who pray to Him.
        Hévénu shalom . . .

397 Danny Daniels
© 1982 Mercy Music / Thankyou Music

Hold me Lord, in Your arms,
Fill me Lord with Your Spirit.
Touch my heart with Your love,
Let my life glorify Your name.

Singing Alleluia, singing Alleluia,
Singing Alleluia, singing Alleluia,
Alleluia, Allelu.
Alleluia, Allelu.

398 Keith Green
© 1982 Birdwing Music /
Mightywind Music / Cherry Lane Music Ltd

How I love You,
You are the One,
You are the One,
How I love You,
You are the One for me.

1 I was so lost
But You showed the way,
'Cause You are the Way.
I was so lost
But You showed the way to me!
        How I love You . . .

2 I was lied to
But You told the truth,
'Cause You are the Truth.
I was lied to
But You showed the truth to me!
        How I love You . . .

3 I was dying
But You gave me life,
'Cause You are the Life.
I was dying
And You gave Your life for me!

        How I love You,
        You are the One,
        You are the One,
        How I love You,
        You are the One,
        God's risen Son.
        You are the One for me!

4 Hallelujah!
You are the One,
You are the One.
Hallelujah!
You are the One for me!
        How I love You . . .

399

1 **How lovely is thy dwelling place,**
O Lord of hosts, to me.
My soul is longing and fainting
The courts of the Lord to see.
My heart and flesh, they are singing
For joy to the living God.
How lovely is Thy dwelling place,
O Lord of hosts, to me.

2 Even the sparrow finds a home
Where he can settle down.
And the swallow, she can build a nest
Where she may lay her young
Within the courts of the Lord of hosts,
My King, my Lord, and my God.
And happy are those who are dwelling
where
The song of praise is sung.

3 And I'd rather be a door-keeper
And only stay a day,
Than live the life of a sinner
And have to stay away.
For the Lord is shining as the sun,
And the Lord, He's like a shield;
And no good thing does He withhold
From those who walk His way.

4 How lovely is thy dwelling place,
O Lord of hosts, to me.
My soul is longing and fainting
The courts of the Lord to see.
My heart and flesh, they are singing
For joy to the living God.
How lovely is thy dwelling place,
O Lord of hosts, to me.

400
Phil Rogers
© 1982 Thankyou Music

How precious, O Lord,
Is Your unfailing love;
We find refuge
In the shadow of Your wings.
We feast, Lord Jesus,
On the abundance of Your house
And drink from Your river of delights.

With You is the fountain of life,
In Your light we see light,
With You is the fountain of life,
In Your light we see light.

401

How great is our God,
How great is His name,
How great is His love
Forever the same.

He rolled back the waters
Of the mighty Red Sea,
And He said, I'll never leave you,
Put your trust in me.

402

1 **'How shall they hear,' who have not
heard**
News of a Lord who loved and came;
Nor known His reconciling word,
Nor learned to trust the Saviour's name?

2 'To all the world,' to every place,
Neighbours and friends and far-off lands,
Preach the good news of saving grace;
Go while the great commission stands.

3 'Whom shall I send?' Who hears the call,
Constant in prayer, through toil and pain,
Telling of one who died for all,
To bring a lost world home again?

4 'Lord, here am I:' Your fire impart
To this poor cold self-centred soul;
Touch but my lips, my hands, my heart,
And make a world for Christ my goal.

5 Spirit of love, within us move:
Spirit of truth, in power come down!
So shall they hear and find and prove
Christ is their life, their joy, their crown.

403
J.D. Burns, 1823–64
Altered © 1986 Horrobin/Leavers

1 **Hushed was the evening hymn,**
The temple courts were dark;
The lamp was burning dim
Before the sacred ark,
When suddenly a voice divine
Rang through the silence of the shrine.

2 The old man, meek and mild,
The priest of Israel, slept;
His watch the temple child,
The little Samuel, kept:
And what from Eli's sense was sealed
The Lord to Hannah's son revealed.

3 O give me Samuel's ear,
The open ear, O Lord,
Alive and quick to hear
Each whisper of Your word—
Like him to answer at Your call,
And to obey You first of all.

4 O give me Samuel's heart,
A lowly heart, that waits
To serve and play the part
You show us at Your gates
By day and night, a heart that still
Moves at the breathing of Your will.

5 O give me Samuel's mind,
A sweet, unmurmuring faith,
Obedient and resigned
To You in life and death,
That I may read with childlike eyes
Truths that are hidden from the wise.

404
Dave Bilbrough
© 1983 Thankyou Music

I am a new creation,
No more in condemnation,
Here in the grace of God I stand.

My heart is over-flowing,
My love just keeps on growing,
Here in the grace of God I stand.

And I will praise You Lord,
Yes I will praise You Lord,
And I will sing of all that You have done.

A joy that knows no limit,
A lightness in my spirit,
Here in the grace of God I stand.

405
Chris A. Bowater
© 1986 Word Music (UK)

1 **I am not mine own,**
I've been bought with a price.
Precious blood of Christ,
I am not mine own.

2 I belong to You,
I've been bought with a price.
Precious blood of Christ,
I belong to You.

3 How could I ever say
'I will choose another way',
Knowing the price that's paid;
Precious blood of Christ.

406
Dora Greenwell, 1821–82 altd.
altered © 1987 Horrobin/Leavers

1 **I am not skilled to understand**
What God has willed, what God has
planned;
I only know at His right hand
Stands One Who is my Saviour!

2 I take Him at His word indeed:
'Christ died for sinners,' this I read;
And in my heart I find a need
Of Him to be my Saviour!

3 That He should leave His place on high,
And come for sinful man to die,
You count it strange? so once did I,
Before I knew my Saviour!

4 And O that He fulfilled may see
The glory of His life in me.
And with His work contented be,
As I with my dear Saviour!

5 Yea, living, dying, let me bring
My life, to Him an offering
That He Who lives to be my King
Once died to be my Saviour.

407
Chris A. Bowater
© 1981 Word Music (UK)

I confess that Jesus Christ is Lord,
I confess that Jesus Christ is Lord.
He's omnipotent, magnificent,
All glorious, victorious;
I confess that Jesus Christ is Lord.

408
Chris A. Bowater
© 1981 Springtide / Word Music

I delight greatly in the Lord,
My soul rejoices in my God.
I delight greatly in the Lord,
My soul rejoices in my God.

For He has clothed me with garments of
salvation
And arrayed me in a robe of righteousness;
He has clothed me with garments of
salvation
And arrayed me in a robe of righteousness.

409

Alfred B. Smith and Eugene Clarke
© Universal Songs / Cherry Pie Music

1 **I do not know what lies ahead,**
The way I cannot see;
Yet one stands near to be my guide,
He'll show the way to me:

I know who holds the future,
And He'll guide me with His hand,
With God things don't just happen,
Ev'rything by Him is planned;
So as I face tomorrow
With its problems large and small,
I'll trust the God of miracles,
Give to Him my all.

2 I do not know how many days
Of life are mine to spend;
But one who knows and cares for me
Will keep me to the end:
I know who holds . . .

3 I do not know the course ahead,
What joys and griefs are there;
But one is near who fully knows,
I'll trust His loving care:
I know who holds . . .

410

Mick Ray
© 1978 Thankyou Music

1 **I get so excited, Lord, ev'ry time I**
   realize
I'm forgiven, I'm forgiven.
Jesus Lord, You've done it all,
You've paid the price.
I'm forgiven, I'm forgiven.

Hallelujah, Lord,
My heart just fills with praise,
My feet start dancing, my hands rise up,
And my lips they bless Your name.
I'm forgiven, I'm forgiven, I'm forgiven.
I'm forgiven, I'm forgiven, I'm forgiven.

2 Living in Your presence, Lord, is life itself.
I'm forgiven, I'm forgiven.
With the past behind, grace for today
And a hope to come.
I'm forgiven, I'm forgiven.
Hallelujah . . .

411

Arthur Tanous
© 1984 Jordan Music
Copyright control

I just want to praise You,
Lift my hands and say: 'I love You.'
You are ev'rything to me
And I exalt Your holy name on high.

412

Carl Tuttle
© 1982 Mercy Music / Thankyou Music

1 **I give You all the honour**
And praise that's due Your name,
For You are the King of Glory,
The Creator of all things.

And I worship You,
I give my life to You,
I fall down on my knees.
Yes, I worship You,
I give my life to You,
I fall down on my knees.

2 As Your Spirit moves upon me now
You meet my deepest need,
And I lift my hands up to Your throne,
Your mercy, I've received.
And I worship . . .

3 You have broken chains that bound me,
You've set this captive free,
I will lift my voice to praise Your name
For all eternity.
And I worship . . .

413

Dave Moody
© 1984 C.A. Music (USA) / Word Music (UK)

I hear the sound of the army of the
   Lord,
I hear the sound of the army of the Lord.
It's the sound of praise,
It's the sound of war,
The army of the Lord,
The army of the Lord,
The army of the Lord is marching on.

414

Eddie Espinosa
© 1982 Mercy Music / Thankyou Music

1 **I lift my hands,**
I raise my voice,
I give my heart to You my Lord
And I rejoice.
There are many, many reasons why I do the
        things I do,
O but most of all, I praise You,
Most of all I praise You,
Jesus, most of all I praise You because
        You're You.

2 I lift my hands,
I raise my voice,
I give my life to You my Lord
And I rejoice.
There are many, many reasons why I do the
        things I do,
O but most of all, I love You,
Most of all I love You,
Jesus, most of all I love You because You're
        You.

3 I lift my hands,
I raise my voice,
I give my love to You my Lord
And I rejoice.
There are many, many reasons why I love
        You like I do,
O but most of all, I love You,
Most of all I love You,
Jesus, most of all I love You because You're
        You.

415

Rich Cook
© 1976 Cherry Pie Music /
Universal Songs B.V.

I live, I live because He is risen,
I live, I live with power over sin.
I live, I live because He is risen,
I live, I live to worship Him.

Thank You Jesus, thank You Jesus,
Because You're alive,
Because You're alive,
Because You're alive I live.

416

© Timothy Dudley-Smith, b. 1926

1 **I lift my eyes**
To the quiet hills
In the press of a busy day;
As green hills stand
In a dusty land
So God is my strength and stay.

2 I lift my eyes
To the quiet hills
To a calm that is mine to share;
Secure and still
In the Father's will
And kept by the Father's care.

3 I lift up my eyes
To the quiet hills
With a prayer as I turn to sleep;
By day, by night,
Through the dark and light
My Shepherd will guard His sheep.

4 I lift up my eyes
To the quiet hills
And my heart to the Father's throne;
In all my ways
To the end of days
The Lord will preserve His own.

417

John Lai
© 1982 Mercy Music / Thankyou Music

1 **I receive You, O Spirit of love,**
How I need Your healing from above,
I receive You, I receive You,
I receive Your healing from above.

2 I can feel You, touching me right now,
Come reveal Your power on me now,
I can feel You, I can feel You,
I can feel Your power on me now,
I can feel Your power on me now.

418

Paul Armstrong
© 1980 Springtide / Word Music

1 **I receive Your love,**
I receive Your love,
In my heart I receive Your love, O Lord.
I receive Your love
By Your Spirit within me,
I receive, I receive Your love.

2 I confess Your love,
I confess Your love,
In my heart I confess Your love, O Lord.
I confess Your love
By Your Spirit within me,
I confess, I confess Your love.

419

Isaac Watts, 1674–1932

1 **I sing the almighty power of God,**
That made the mountains rise,
That spread the flowing seas abroad,
And built the lofty skies.

2 I sing the wisdom that ordained
The sun to rule the day;
The moon shines full at His command,
And all the stars obey.

3 I sing the goodness of the Lord,
That filled the earth with food;
He formed the creatures with His word,
And then pronounced them good.

4 Creatures, as numerous as they be,
Are subject to His care;
There's not a place where we can flee
But God is present there.

5 Lord, how Thy wonders are displayed
Where'er I turn mine eye,
If I survey the ground I tread,
Or gaze upon the sky.

6 God's hand is my perpetual guard,
He guides me with His eye;
Why should I then forget the Lord,
Whose love is ever nigh?

420

Carl Tuttle and John Wimber
© 1982 Mercy Music / Thankyou Music

1 **I sing a new song to the Lord, my God.**
I lift my voice to Jesus, the King.
And I worship You, I worship You,
I worship You, I worship You.

2 I bow down my face at the footstool of the
   Lamb,
I lay down my life at the alter of God.
And I worship You, I worship You,
I worship You, I worship You.

421

Charles H. Gabriel, 1858–1932

1 **I stand amazed in the presence**
Of Jesus the Nazarene,
And wonder how He could love me,
A sinner, condemned, unclean.

How marvellous! How wonderful!
And my song shall ever be;
How marvellous! How wonderful!
Is my Saviour's love for me!

2 For me it was in the garden
He prayed – 'Not My will, but Thine':
He had tears for His own griefs,
But sweat drops of blood for mine.
How marvellous! . . .

3 In pity angels beheld Him,
And came from the world of light
To comfort Him in the sorrows
He bore for my soul that night.
How marvellous! . . .

4 He took my sins and my sorrows,
He made them His very own;
He bore the burden to Calvary,
And suffered, and died alone.
How marvellous! . . .

5 When with the ransomed in glory
His face I at last shall see,
'Twill be my joy through the ages
To sing of His love for me.
How marvellous! . . .

422

Mavis Ford
© 1980 Springtide / Word Music

I stand before the presence
Of the Lord God of hosts,
A child of my Father
And an heir of His grace,
For Jesus paid the debt for me,
The veil was torn in two,
And the Holy of Holies
Has become my dwelling place.

423

John Kennett
© 1980 Thankyou Music

I want to learn to appreciate You
Lord in every way,
I want to learn to walk with You
Lord, day by day,
With You always there to guide me,
Hand in hand,
There beside me,
Walking in the Spirit day by day.

424

Dave Fellingham
© 1982 Thankyou Music

I will rejoice, I will rejoice,
I will rejoice in the Lord with my whole
  heart.
I will rejoice, I will rejoice,
I will rejoice in the Lord.

You anoint my head with oil,
And my cup surely overflows.
Goodness and love shall follow me
All the days that I dwell in Your house.

425

Phil Potter
© 1981 Thankyou Music

I will sing about Your love,
I will magnify Your name.
I will be glad and rejoice in You,
I will praise You again,
Praise the Lord, lift your voices high.
Praise the Lord,
Tell them He's alive.
Praise the Lord, praise the Lord.

426

© 1985 Andy Silver

I will wait upon the Lord,
My hope is all in Him.
He only is my rock and strength,
My refuge is in God.
I will trust Him at all times,
Pour out my heart to Him.

He only is my rock and strength,
My refuge is in God.
I will wait upon the Lord,
My hope is all in Him;
He only is my rock and strength,
My refuge is in God.

427

Isaac Watts, 1674–1748

1 **I'll praise my Maker while I've breath;**
  And when my voice is lost in death,
  Praise shall employ my nobler pow'rs:
  My days of praise shall ne'er be past,
  While life, and thought, and being last,
  Or immortality endures.

2 Happy the man whose hopes rely
  On Israel's God! He made the sky,
  And earth, and sea, with all their train:
  His truth for ever stands secure;
  He saves th'oppressed, He feeds the poor,
  And none shall find His promise vain.

3 The Lord gives eyesight to the blind;
  The Lord supports the fainting mind;
  He sends the lab'ring conscience peace;
  He helps the stranger in distress,
  The widow, and the fatherless,
  And grants the pris'ner sweet release.

4 I'll praise Him while He lends me breath;
  And when my voice is lost in death,
  Praise shall employ my nobler pow'rs:
  My days of praise shall ne'er be past,
  While life, and thought, and being last,
  Or immortality endures.

428

Copyright control

I will rejoice in You and be glad,
I will extol Your love more than wine,
Draw me after You and let us run together,
I will rejoice in You and be glad.

429

Copyright control

I'm confident of this very thing
That he who has begun a good work in you
He will perform it until the day of
    Jesus Christ,
He will perform it until the day of
    Jesus Christ,
He will perform it until the day of
    Jesus Christ.

430

Tony Humphries
© 1980 Thankyou Music

I'm redeemed, Yes I am,
By the blood of the Lamb,
Jesus Christ has done it all for me.
I am His, He is mine,
I'm part of the royal vine,
All my sins were washed away at Calvary.

Once I was lost, I had nowhere to go,
My life was just a lonely round of sin.
Till Jesus said to me,
By My blood shed on the tree
I've paid the price,
Brought you back,
You're mine,
Oh what a friend!

I'm redeemed, Yes I am,
By the blood of the Lamb,
Jesus Christ has done it all for me.
I am His, He is mine,
I'm part of the royal vine,
All my sins were washed away at Calvary.

431

Graham Kendrick
© 1986 Thankyou Music

I'm special because God has loved me,
For He gave the best thing that He had to
    save me.
His own Son Jesus, crucified to take the
    blame,
For all the bad things I have done.

Thank You Jesus, thank You Lord,
For loving me so much.
I know I don't deserve anything,
Help me feel Your love right now
To know deep in my heart that I'm Your
    special friend.

432

Andy and Becky Silver
© 1987 Andy Silver

I am trusting in You, O God,
In the power of Your name;
And I know that as long as I wait
For You my hope will not be in vain.
There may be problems,
There may be pain,
But my hope will not be in vain.

433

Randy Speir
© Integrity's Hosanna! Music

**In Him we live and move and have our
    being,**
In Him we live and move and have our
    being.
Make a joyful noise, sing unto the Lord,
Tell Him of your love, dance before Him.
Make a joyful noise, sing unto the Lord,
Tell Him of your love, Hallelujah!

434

David Graham
© C.A. Music (USA), Word Music (UK)

**In moments like these, I sing out a
    song,**
I sing out a love song to Jesus,
In moments like these, I lift up my hands,
I lift up my hands to the Lord,
Singing I love You Lord,
Singing I love You Lord,
Singing I love You Lord,
I love You.

435

John Oxenham, 1852–1941
Copyright control

1   **In Christ there is no East or West,**
    In Him no South or North,
    But one great fellowship of love
    Throughout the whole wide earth.

2   In Him shall true hearts everywhere
    Their high communion find:
    His service is the golden cord
    Close-binding all mankind.

3   Join hands then, brothers of the faith,
    Whate'er your race may be!
    Who serves my Father as a son
    Is surely kin to me.

4   In Christ now meet both East and West,
    In Him meet South and North,
    All Christly souls are one in Him,
    Throughout the whole wide earth.

436

© Gordon Brattle

In my need Jesus found me,
Put His strong arm around me,
Brought me safe home,
Into the shelter of the fold.

Gracious Shepherd that sought me,
Precious life-blood that bought me;
Out of the night,
Into the light and near to God.

437 Christina Georgina Rossetti, 1830–94

1 **In the bleak mid-winter**
Frosty wind made moan,
Earth stood hard as iron,
Water like a stone;
Snow had fallen, snow on snow,
Snow on snow,
In the bleak mid-winter,
Long ago.

2 Our God, heaven cannot hold Him,
Nor earth sustain;
Heaven and earth shall flee away
When He comes to reign;
In the bleak mid-winter
A stable-place sufficed
The Lord God Almighty,
Jesus Christ.

3 Angels and archangels
May have gathered there,
Cherubim and seraphim
Thronged the air;
But His mother only,
In her maiden bliss,
Worshipped the Belovèd
With a kiss.

4 What can I give Him,
Poor as I am?
If I were a shepherd,
I would bring a lamb;
If I were a wise man,
I would do my part;
Yet what I can I give Him –
Give my heart.

438 Graham Kendrick
© 1986 Thankyou Music

1 **In the tomb so cold they laid Him,**
Death its victim claimed.
Powers of hell they could not hold Him,
Back to life He came!

   Christ is risen, (Christ is risen),
   Death has been conquered,
     (Death has been conquered),
   Christ is risen, (Christ is risen),
   He shall reign for ever!

2 Hell had spent its fury on Him,
Left Him crucified.
Yet by blood He boldly conquered
Sin and death defied.
   Christ is risen . . .

3 Now the fear of death is broken,
Love has won the crown.
Prisoners of the darkness listen,
Walls are tumbling down.
   Christ is risen . . .

4 Raised from death to heav'n ascending
Love's exalted King.
Let His song of joy unending
Through the nations ring!
   Christ is risen . . .

439 tr. E.M.G Reed
Kingsway Carol Book

1 **Infant holy,**
Infant lowly,
For His bed a cattle stall;
Oxen lowing,
Little knowing
Christ the babe is Lord of all.
Swift are winging
Angels singing,
Nowells ringing,
Tidings bringing,
Christ the babe is Lord of all,
Christ the babe is Lord of all.

2 Flocks were sleeping,
Shepherds keeping
Vigil till the morning new.
Saw the glory,
Heard the story,
Tidings of a gospel true.
Thus rejoicing,
Free from sorrow,
Praises voicing,
Greet the morrow,
Christ the babe was born for you!
Christ the babe was born for you!

440 © 1987 Anne Horrobin and Stephen Poxon

1 **Is this the church of our God?**
Is this the church of the Word?
Is this the church of His Son Jesus Christ?
Is this the church of His Spirit?

2 If we're dependant on Him,
If we believe God's own Word,
If we're redeemed by the blood of His Son,
If we are filled with His Spirit.

3 Then this is the church of our God,
Then this is the church of His Word,
Then this is the church of His Son
      Jesus Christ,
Then this is the church of our Lord.

4 Yes, this is the church of our God,
Yes, this is the church of His Word,
Yes, this is the church of His Son
    Jesus Christ,
Yes, this is the church of our Lord.

441 John Wimber
© 1980 Maranatha! Music, USA /
Word Music (UK)

1 **Isn't He beautiful,**
Beautiful, isn't He?
Prince of Peace,
Son of God,
Isn't He?
Isn't He wonderful,
Wonderful, isn't He?
Counsellor,
Almighty God,
Isn't He, isn't He,
Isn't He, isn't He?
Isn't He?

2 Yes You are beautiful,
Beautiful, yes you are!
Prince of Peace,
Son of God,
Yes You are!
Yes You are wonderful,
Wonderful, yes You are!
Counsellor,
Almighty God,
Yes You are, yes You are,
Yes You are, yes You are,
Yes You are!

442 E.H. Sears, 1810–76
© in this version Jubilate Hymns

1 **It came upon the midnight clear,**
That glorious song of old,
From angels bending near the earth
To touch their harps of gold:
'Peace on the earth, goodwill to men
From heaven's all-gracious king!'
The world in solemn stillness lay
To hear the angels sing.

2 With sorrow brought by sin and strife
The world has suffered long,
And, since the angels sang, have passed
Two thousand years of wrong:
For man at war with man hears not
The love-song which they bring:
O hush the noise, you men of strife,
And hear the angels sing!

3 And those whose journey now is hard,
Whose hope is burning low,
Who tread the rocky path of life
With painful steps and slow:
O listen to the news of love
Which makes the heavens ring!
O rest beside the weary road
And hear the angels sing!

4 And still the days are hastening on—
By prophets seen of old—
Towards the fulness of the time
When comes the age foretold:
Then earth and heaven renewed shall see
The Prince of Peace, their king;
And all the world repeat the song
Which now the angels sing.

443 H.L. Turner

1 **It may be at morn, when the day is
    awaking**
When sunlight through darkness and
    shadow is breaking,
That Jesus will come in the fulness of glory,
To receive from the world 'His own'.

    O Lord Jesus, how long?
    How long ere we shout the glad song?
    Christ returneth, Hallelujah! Hallelujah!
    Amen,
    Hallelujah! Amen.

2 It may be at mid-day it may be at twilight,
It may be, perchance, that the blackness of
    midnight
Will burst into light in the blaze of His glory,
When Jesus receives 'His own'.
    O Lord Jesus . . .

3 While hosts cry Hosanna, from heaven
    descending,
With glorified saints and the angels
    attending,
With grace on His brow, like a halo of glory,
Will Jesus receive 'His own'.
    O Lord Jesus . . .

4 Oh, joy! Oh, delight! Should we go without
    dying;
No sickness, no sadness, no dread and no
    crying;
Caught up through the clouds with our Lord
    into glory,
When Jesus receives 'His own'.
    O Lord Jesus . . .

444 © 1964 C. Simmonds

1 **I want to walk with Jesus Christ,**
All the days I live of this life on earth,
To give to Him complete control
Of body and of soul:

*Follow Him, follow Him, yield your life to
Him,*
*He has conquered death, He is King of
kings.*
Accept the joy which He gives to those
Who yield their lives to Him.

2 I want to learn to speak to Him,
To pray to Him, confess my sin,
To open my life and let Him in,
For joy will then be mine:
Follow Him, follow Him . . .

3 I want to learn to speak of Him,
My life must show that He lives in me,
My deeds, my thoughts, my words must
speak
All of His love for me:
Follow Him, follow Him . . .

4 I want to learn to read His Word,
For this is how I know the way,
To live my life as pleases Him,
In holiness and joy:
Follow Him, follow Him . . .

5 O Holy Spirit of the Lord,
Enter now into this heart of mine,
Take full control of my selfish will
And make me wholly Thine:
Follow Him, follow Him . . .

445 Sally Ellis
© 1980 Thankyou Music

It is no longer I that liveth
But Christ that liveth in me,
It is no longer I that liveth
But Christ that liveth in me.

He lives, He lives,
Jesus is alive in me.
It is no longer I that liveth
But Christ that liveth in me.

446 Chris A. Bowater
© 1981 Springtide / Word Music (UK)

Jesus at Your name we bow the knee.
Jesus at Your name we bow the knee.
Jesus at Your name we bow the knee,
And acknowledge You as Lord.
You are the Christ You are the Lord.

Through Your Spirit in our lives
We know who You are;
You are the Christ You are the Lord.
Through Your Spirit in our lives
We know who You are.

447 Lyra Davidica, 1708

1 **Jesus Christ is risen today,** *Hallelujah!*
Our triumphant holy day, *Hallelujah!*
Who did once, upon the cross, *Hallelujah!*
Suffer to redeem our loss. *Hallelujah!*

2 Hymns of praise then let us sing, *Hallelujah!*
Unto Christ, our heavenly King, *Hallelujah!*
Who endured the cross and grave,
Hallelujah!
Sinners to redeem and save. *Hallelujah!*

3 But the pains which He endured, *Hallelujah!*
Our salvation have procured, *Hallelujah!*
Now in heaven above He's King, *Hallelujah!*
Where the angels ever sing: *Hallelujah!*

448 Jonathan Wallis
© 1983 Thankyou Music

1 **Jesus has sat down at God's right hand,**
He is reigning now on David's throne.
God has placed all things beneath His feet,
His enemies will be His footstool.

*For the government is now upon His
shoulder,*
*For the government is now upon His
shoulder,*
*And of the increase of His government
and peace*
There will be no end,
There will be no end,
There will be no end.

2 God has exalted Him on high,
Given Him a name above all names.
Every knee will bow and tongue confess
That Jesus Christ is Lord.
For the government . . .

3 Jesus is now living in His church,
  Men who have been purchased by His
      blood.
  They will serve their God, a royal
      priesthood,
  And they will reign on earth.
      For the government . . .

4 Sounds the trumpet, good news to the poor,
  Captives will go free, the blind will see,
  The kingdom of this world will soon
      become
  The kingdom of out God.
      For the government . . .

449

1 **Jesus is King and I will extol Him,**
  Give Him the glory and honour His name.
  He reigns on high, enthroned in the
      heavens,
  Word of the Father, exalted for us.

2 We have a hope that is steadfast and certain,
  Gone through the curtain and touching the
      throne.
  We have a Priest who is there interceding,
  Pouring His grace on our lives day by day.

3 We come to Him, our Priest and Apostle,
  Clothed in His glory and bearing His name,
  Laying our lives with gladness before Him;
  Filled with His Spirit we worship the King.

4 O holy One, our hearts do adore You;
  Thrilled with Your goodness we give You
      our praise.
  Angels in light with worship surround Him,
  Jesus, our Saviour, for ever the same.

450

1 **Jesus is Lord of all,**
  Satan is under His feet,
  Jesus is reigning on high
  And all pow'r is given to Him
  In heaven and earth.

2 We are joined to Him,
  Satan is under our feet,
  We are seated on high
  And all authority is given
  To us through Him.

3 One day we'll be like Him,
  Perfect in every way,
  Chosen to be His bride,
  Ruling and reigning with Him
  For evermore.

451

Jesus, I worship You,
Worship, honour and adore Your lovely
    name.
Jesus, I worship You,
Lord of lords and King of kings,
I worship You,
From a thankful heart I sing;
I worship You.

452

Jesus is the Lord, Jesus the Lord reigns,
We will take the kingdoms of this world in
    His name.
Every tribe and nation, every situation,
Must delcare that Jesus is the Lord.

For the Lord our God has delivered Him
    from death
And established Jesus as Lord,
He has given Him the power over all that He
    has made,
For our God has made Him Christ the Lord.

453

1 **Jesus, Jesus,**
  You are my Lord and my heart's desire.
  Jesus, Jesus,
  Keep us in Your love.

2 Jesus, Jesus,
  You are my King and my Sovereign Master.
  Jesus, Jesus,
  I will serve Your Lord.

454

1 **Jesus lives! thy terrors now**
  Can, O death, no more appal us;
  Jesus lives! by this we know
  Thou, O grave, canst not enthral us.
      Hallelujah!

2 Jesus lives! henceforth is death
But the gate of life immortal;
This shall calm our trembling breath
When we pass its gloomy portal.
Hallelujah!

3 Jesus lives! for us He died;
Then, alone to Jesus living,
Pure in heart may we abide,
Glory to our Saviour giving.
Hallelujah!

4 Jesus lives! our hearts know well
Naught from us His love shall sever;
Life, nor death, nor powers of hell
Tear us from His keeping ever.
Hallelujah!

5 Jesus lives! to Him the throne
Over all the world is given;
May we go where He is gone,
Rest and reign with Him in heaven.
Hallelujah!

455 Chris A. Bowater
© 1982 Springtide Music / Word Music (UK)

Jesus, Jesus, Jesus,
Your love has melted my heart.
Jesus, Jesus, Jesus,
Your love has melted my heart.

456 © Timothy Dudley-Smith, b. 1926

1 **Jesus, Prince and Saviour,**
Lord of life who died:
Christ, the friend of sinners,
Sinners crucified.
For a lost world's ransom
All Himself He gave,
Lay at last death's victim
Lifeless in the grave.

Lord of life triumphant,
Risen now to reign!
King of endless ages,
Jesus lives again!

2 In His power and Godhead
Every victory won,
Pain and passion ended,
All His purpose done:
Christ the Lord is risen!
Sighs and sorrows past,
Death's dark night is over,
Morning comes at last!
Lord of life . . .

3 Resurrection morning!
Sinners' bondage freed.
Christ the Lord is risen—
He is risen indeed!
Jesus, Prince and Saviour,
Lord of life who died,
Christ the King of glory
Now is glorified!
Lord of life . . .

457 Graham Kendrick
© 1986 Thankyou Music

1 **Jesus put this song into our hearts,**
Jesus put this song into our hearts.
It's a song of joy no-one can take away
Jesus put this song into our hearts.

2 Jesus taught us how to live in harmony,
Jesus taught us how to live in harmony,
Different faces, different races, He made us
one,
Jesus taught us how to live in harmony.

3 Jesus taught us how to be a family,
Jesus taught us how to be a family,
Loving one another with the love that He
gives,
Jesus taught us how to be a family.

4 Jesus turned our sorrow into dancing,
Jesus turned our sorrow into dancing,
Changed our tears of sadness into rivers of
joy,
Jesus turned our sorrow into a dance.

458 Translated from Urdu by D. Monahan, 1906–1957
© The Methodist Church,
Division of Education and Youth

1 **Jesus the Lord said: 'I am the bread,**
The bread of life for mankind am I,
The bread of life for mankind am I,
The bread of life for mankind am I.'
Jesus the Lord said: 'I am the bread,
The bread of life for mankind am I.'

2 Jesus the Lord said: 'I am the way,
The true and living way am I,
The true and living way am I,
The true and living way am I.'
Jesus the Lord said: 'I am the way,
The true and living way am I.'

3 Jesus the Lord said: 'I am the light,
The one true light of the world am I,
The one true light of the world am I,
The one true light of the world am I.'
Jesus the Lord said: 'I am the light,
The one true light of the world am I.'

4 Jesus the Lord said: 'I am the shepherd,
The one good shepherd of the sheep am I,
The one good shepherd of the sheep am I,
The one good shepherd of the sheep am I.'
Jesus the Lord said: 'I am the shepherd,
The one good shepherd of the sheep am I.'

5 Jesus the Lord said: 'I am the life,
The resurrection and the life am I,
The resurrection and the life am I,
The resurrection and the life am I.'
Jesus the Lord said: 'I am the life,
The resurrection and the life am I.'

459
Marilyn Baker
© 1981 Word Music (UK)

Jesus, You are changing me.
By Your Spirit You're making me like You.
Jesus, You're transforming me,
That Your loveliness may be seen in all I do.

You are the Potter and I am the clay
Help me to be willing to let You have Your
way,
Jesus, You are changing me
As I let You reign supreme within my heart.

460
Dave Fellingham
© 1985 Thankyou Music

**Jesus, You are the radiance of the
Father's glory,**
You are the Son, the appointed heir,
Through whom all things are made.
You are the One who sustains all things
By Your powerful word.
You have purified us from sin,
You are exalted, O Lord,
Exalted, O Lord, to the right hand of God.

Crowned with glory,
Crowned with honour,
We worship You.

461
Isaac Watts, 1674–1748

1 **Join all the glorious names**
Of wisdom, love, and power,
That ever mortals knew,
That angels ever bore:
All are too mean to speak His worth,
Too mean to set my Saviour forth.

2 Great Prophet of my God,
My tongue would bless Thy Name:
By Thee the joyful news
Of our salvation came:
The joyful news of sins forgiven,
Of hell subdued and peace with heaven.

3 Jesus, my great High Priest,
Offered His blood, and died;
My guilty conscience seeks
No sacrifice beside:
His powerful blood did once atone,
And now it pleads before the throne.

4 My Saviour and my Lord,
My Conqueror and my King,
Thy sceptre and Thy sword,
Thy reigning grace I sing:
Thine is the power; behold, I sit
In willing bonds beneath Thy feet.

5 Now let my soul arise,
And tread the tempter down:
My Captain leads me forth
To conquest and a crown:
March on, nor fear to win the day,
Though death and hell obstruct the way.

6 Should all the hosts of death,
And powers of hell unknown,
Put their most dreadful forms
Of rage and malice on,
I shall be safe; for Christ displays
Superior power and guardian grace.

462
George Herbert, 1593–1633

1 **King of glory, King of peace,**
I will love Thee;
And, that love may never cease,
I will move Thee.
Thou hast granted my request,
Thou hast heard me;
Thou didst note my working breast,
Thou hast spared me.

2 Wherefore with my utmost art
I will sing Thee,
And the cream of all my heart
I will bring Thee.
Though my sins against me cried,
Thou didst clear me;
And alone, when they replied,
Thou didst hear me.

3 Seven whole days, not one in seven,
  I will praise Thee;
  In my heart, though not in heaven,
  I can raise Thee.
  Small it is, in this poor sort
  To enrol Thee:
  E'en eternity's too short
  To extol Thee.

463
Sophie Conty and Naomi Batya
© 1980 Maranatha Music / Word Music (UK)

King of kings and Lord of lords,
Glory, Hallelujah!
King of kings and Lord of lords,
Glory, Hallelujah!
Jesus, Prince of Peace,
Glory, Hallelujah!
Jesus, Prince of Peace,
Glory, Hallelujah!

464
J.H. Newman, 1801–90

1 **Lead kindly Light, amid th'encircling
    gloom,**
    Lead Thou me on;
  The night is dark, and I am far from home;
    Lead Thou me on.
  Keep Thou my feet; I do not ask to see
  The distant scene; one step enough for me.

2 I was not ever thus, nor prayed that Thou
    Shouldst lead me on;
  I loved to choose and see my path; but now
    Lead Thou me on.
  I loved the garish day, and, spite of fears,
  Pride ruled my will: remember not past
    years.

3 So long Thy power has blest me, sure it still
    Will lead me on
  O'er moor and fen, o'er crag and torrent, till
    The night is gone;
  And with the morn those angel faces smile
  Which I have loved long since, and lost
    awhile.

465
James Edmeston, 1791–1867

1 **Lead us, heavenly Father, lead us**
  O'er the world's tempestuous sea;
  Guard us, guide us, keep us, feed us,
  For we have no help but Thee;
  Yet possessing ev'ry blessing
  If our God our Father be.

2 Saviour, breathe forgiveness o'er us;
  All our weakness Thou dost know:
  Thou didst tread this earth before us,
  Thou didst feel its keenest woe;
  Lone and dreary, faint and weary,
  Through the desert Thou didst go.

3 Spirit of our God, descending,
  Fill our hearts with heav'nly joy,
  Love with ev'ry passion blending,
  Pleasure that can never cloy:
  Thus provided, pardoned, guided,
  Nothing can our peace destroy.

466
C. Wesley, 1707–88
© in this version Jubilate Hymns

1 **Let saints on earth together sing**
  With those whose work is done;
  For all the servants of our King
  In earth and heaven, are one.

2 One family, we live in Him,
  One church above, beneath,
  Though now divided by the stream,
  The narrow stream of death.

3 One army of the living God,
  To His command we bow;
  Part of His host have crossed the flood
  And part are crossing now.

4 But all unite in Christ their head,
  And love to sing His praise:
  Lord of the living and the dead,
  Direct our earthly ways!

5 So shall we join our friends above
  Who have obtained the prize;
  And on the eagle wings of love
  To joys celestial rise.

467

Graham Kendrick
© 1984 Thankyou Music

Let God arise, and let His enemies be
scattered;
And let those who hate Him flee before Him.
Let God arise, and let His enemies be
scattered;
And let those who hate Him flee away.

But let the righteous be glad,
Let them exult before God,
Let them rejoice with gladness,
Building up a highway for the King,
We go in the name of the Lord,
Let the shout go up in the name of the Lord.

468

Brent Chambers
© 1979 Scripture in Song /
Thankyou Music

Let our praise to You be as incense,
Let our praise to You be as pillars of Your
throne.
Let our praise to You be as incense,
As we come before You and worship You
alone.

As we see You in Your splendour,
As we gaze upon Your majesty;
As we join the hosts of angels,
And proclaim together Your holiness.

Let our praise to You be as incense,
Let our praise to You be as pillars of Your
throne.
Let our praise to You be as incense,
As we come before You and worship You
alone.

Holy, holy, holy, holy is the Lord!

469

© 1986 Andy Silver

Let us acknowledge the Lord,
Let us press on to acknowledge Him,
Let us acknowledge the Lord.

Let us acknowledge Him
As surely as the sun rises,
He will appear, He will come to us
Like the winter rains,
Like the spring rains
That water the earth.

470

J.E. Seddon 1915–83
© Mavis Seddon/Jubilate Hymns

VERSION 1 (TRADITIONAL)

1 **Let us break bread together on our**
 knees,
 Let us break bread together on our knees:

 When I fall on my knees,
 With my face to the rising sun,
 O Lord, have mercy on me!

2 Let us drink wine together on our knees,
 Let us drink wine together on our knees:
 When I fall . . .

3 Let us praise God together on our knees,
 Let us praise God together on our knees:
 When I fall . . .

VERSION 2

1 Let us praise God together, let us praise;
 Let us praise God together all our days:
 He is faithful in all His ways,
 He is worthy of all our praise,
 His name be exalted on high!

2 Let us seek God together, let us pray;
 Let us seek His forgiveness as we pray:
 He will cleanse us from all sin,
 He will help us the fight to win,
 His name be exalted on high!

3 Let us serve God together, Him obey;
 Let our lives show His goodness through
 each day:
 Christ the Lord is the world's true light—
 Let us serve Him with all our might,
 His name be exalted on high!

471

John Milton, 1608–74

1 **Let us with a gladsome mind**
 Praise the Lord, for He is kind;

 For His mercies shall endure,
 Ever faithful, ever sure.

2 He, with all-commanding might,
 Filled the new-made world with light:
 For His mercies . . .

3 All things living He doth feed,
 His full hand supplies their need:
 For His mercies . . .

4 He His chosen race did bless
 In the wasteland wilderness:
 For His mercies . . .

5 He hath with a piteous eye
Looked upon our misery:
For His mercies . . .

6 Let us, then, with gladsome mind,
Praise the Lord, For He is kind!
For His mercies . . .

472

Lift Jesus higher, lift Jesus higher,
Lift Him up for the world to see.
He said if I be lifted up from the earth
I will draw all men unto me.

473

Lift up your heads to the coming King.
Bow before Him and adore Him,
Sing to His majesty,
Let your praises be pure and holy,
Giving glory to the King of kings.

474

1 **Living under the shadow of His wing**
We find security.
Standing in His presence we will bring
Our worship, worship, worship to the King.

2 Bowed in adoration at His feet
We dwell in harmony.
Voices joined together that repeat,
Worthy, worthy, worthy is the Lamb.

3 Heart to heart embracing in His love
Reveals His purity.
Soaring in my spirit like a dove.
Holy, holy, holy is the Lord.

475
Thomas Kelly, 1769–1854

1 **Look, ye saints, the sight is glorious!**
See the Man of Sorrows now,
From the fight returned victorious,
Every knee to Him shall bow:
Crown Him! Crown Him!
Crown Him! Crown Him!
Crowns become the Victor's brow.

2 Crown the Saviour! angels, crown Him!
Rich the trophies Jesus brings;
In the seat of power enthrone Him,
While the vault of heaven rings:
Crown Him! Crown Him!
Crown Him! Crown Him!
Crown the Saviour King of kings!

3 Sinners in derision crowned Him,
Mocking thus the Saviour's claim;
Saints and angels crowd around Him,
Own His title, praise His name:
Crown Him! Crown Him!
Crown Him! Crown Him!
Spread abroad the Victor's fame.

4 Hark, those bursts of acclamation!
Hark, those loud triumphant chords!
Jesus takes the highest station:
O what joy the sight affords!
Crown Him! Crown Him!
Crown Him! Crown Him!
King of kings, and Lord of lords!

476
G. Bourne, 1840–1925

1 **Lord enthroned in heavenly splendour,**
Glorious first born from the dead,
You alone our strong defender,
Lifting up Your people's head:
Alleluia, alleluia,
Jesus, true and living bread!

2 Prince of life, for us now living,
By Your body souls are healed;
Prince of peace, Your pardon giving,
By Your blood our peace is sealed:
Alleluia, alleluia,
Word of God in flesh revealed.

3 Paschal Lamb! Your offering finished,
Once for all, when You were slain;
In its fulness undiminished
Shall for evermore remain:
Alleluia, alleluia,
Cleansing souls from every stain.

4 Great High Priest of our profession,
Through the veil You entered in,
By Your mighty intercession
Grace and mercy there to win:
Alleluia, alleluia,
Only sacrifice for sin.

5 Life-imparting heavenly manna,
   Stricken rock, with streaming side;
   Heaven and earth, with loud hosanna,
   Worship You, the Lamb who died:
   Alleluia, alleluia,
   Risen, ascended, glorified!

477 W.T. Matson, 1833–1899
© in this version Jubilate Hymns

1 **Lord, I was blind; I could not see**
   In Your marred visage any grace:
   But now the beauty of Your face
   In radiant vision dawns on me.

2 Lord, I was deaf; I could not hear
   The thrilling music of Your voice:
   But now I hear You and rejoice,
   And all Your spoken words are dear.

3 Lord, I was dumb; I could not speak
   The grace and glory of Your name:
   But now as touched with living flame
   My lips will speak for Jesus' sake.

4 Lord, I was dead; I could not move
   My lifeless soul from sin's dark grave:
   But now the power of life You gave
   Has raised me up to know Your love.

5 Lord, You have made the blind to see,
   The deaf to hear, the dumb to speak,
   The dead to live – and now I break
   The chains of my captivity!

478 H. Ernest Nichol, 1862–1926

1 **Lord, it is eventide: the light of day is
   waning;**
   Far o'er the golden land earth's voices faint
   and fall;
   Lowly we pray to You for strength and love
   sustaining,
   Lowly we ask of You Your peace upon us
   all.
   O grant unto our souls –

   *Light that grows not pale with day's
   decrease,
   Love that never can fail till life shall cease;
   Joy no trial can mar, Hope that shines afar,
   Faith serene as a star, and Christ's own
   peace.*

2 Lord, it is eventide: we turn to You for
   healing,
   Like those of Galilee who came at close of
   day;
   Speak to our waiting souls, their hidden
   needs revealing;
   Touch us with hands divine that take our sin
   away.
   O grant unto our souls –
   Light that grows . . .

3 Saviour, You know of every trial and
   temptation,
   Know of the wilfulness and waywardness of
   youth,
   Help us to hold to You, our strength and our
   salvation,
   Help us to find in You the one eternal Truth.
   O grant unto our souls –
   Light that grows . . .

4 Lord, it is eventide: our hearts await Your
   giving,
   Wait for that peace divine that none can take
   away,
   Peace that shall lift our souls to loftier
   heights of living,
   Till we abide with You in everlasting day.
   O grant unto our souls –
   Light that grows . . .

479 J.C. Winslow, 1882–1974
© Mrs. J. Tyrrell

1 **Lord of creation, to You be all praise!**
   Most mighty Your working, most wondrous
   Your ways!
   Your glory and might are beyond us to tell,
   And yet in the heart of the humble You
   dwell.

2 Lord of all power, I give to You my will,
   In joyful obedience Your tasks to fulfil;
   Your bondage is freedom, Your service is
   song,
   And, held in Your keeping, my weakness is
   strong.

3 Lord of all wisdom, I give to You my mind;
   Rich truth that surpasses man's knowledge
   to find,
   What eye has not seen and what ear has not
   heard
   Is taught by Your Spirit and shines from
   Your word.

4   Lord of all bounty, I give You my heart;
    I praise and adore You for all You impart –
    Your love to inspire me, Your counsel to
        guide,
    Your presence to cheer me, whatever
        betide.

5   Lord of all being, I give You my all;
    For if I disown You I stumble and fall,
    But, sworn in glad service Your word to
        obey,
    I walk in Your freedom to the end of the
        way.

480
P. Appleford
© 1960 Josef Weinberger Ltd

1   **Lord Jesus Christ,**
    You have come to us,
    You are one with us,
    Mary's Son.
    Cleansing our souls
    from all their sin,
    Pouring Your love
    And goodness in,
    Jesus, our love
    For You we sing,
    Living Lord.

2   Lord Jesus Christ,
    Now and every day,
    Teach us how to pray,
    Son of God.
    You have commanded
    Us to do
    This in remembrance,
    Lord, of You:
    Into our lives
    Your power breaks through,
    Living Lord.

3   Lord Jesus Christ,
    You have come to us,
    Born as one of us,
    Mary's Son.
    Led out to die
    On Calvary,
    Risen from death
    To set us free,
    Living Lord Jesus,
    Help us see
    You are Lord.

4   Lord Jesus Christ,
    I would come to You,
    Live my life for You,
    Son of God.
    All Your commands
    I know are true,
    Your many gifts
    Will make me new,
    Into my life
    Your power breaks through,
    Living Lord.

481
Graham Kendrick
© 1986 Thankyou Music

Lord have mercy on us,
Come and heal our land,
Cleanse with Your fire,
Heal with Your touch,
Humbly we bow and call upon You now,
O Lord, have mercy on us.
O Lord, have mercy on us.

482
Gerald Markland
© 1978 Kevin Mayhew Ltd

Lord have mercy, Lord have mercy,
Lord have mercy on Your people.

1   Give me the heart of stone within you,
    And I'll give you a heart of flesh.
    Clean water I will use to cleanse all your
        wounds.
    My Spirit I give to you.
        Lord have mercy . . .

2   You'll find Me near the broken-hearted,
    Those crushed in spirit I will save.
    So turn to Me for My pardon is great,
    My word will heal all your wounds.
        Lord have mercy . . .

483
Paul Field
© 1983 Waif / Heath Levy Music

1   **Lord make me a mountain standing tall**
        for You,
    Strong and free and holy, in everything I do.
    Lord, make me a river of water pure and
        sweet,
    Lord, make me the servant of everyone I
        meet.

2 Lord make me a candle with Your light,
Steadfastly unflickering, standing for the
right,
Lord make me a fire burning strong for
You,
Lord, make me be humble in everything I
do.

3 Lord make me a mountain, strong and tall
for You,
Lord make me a fountain of water clear and
new,
Lord make me a shepherd that I may feed
Your sheep,
Lord make me the servant of everyone I
meet.

484 Philip Pusey, 1799–1855, based on
Matthaus Apelles von Löwenstern, 1594–1648

1 **Lord of our life, and God of our
salvation,**
Star of our night, and Hope of every nation,
Hear and receive Thy church's supplication,
Lord God Almighty!

2 Lord, Thou canst help when earthly armour
faileth,
Lord, Thou canst save when sin itself
assaileth,
Lord, o'er Thy church nor death nor hell
prevaileth;
Grant us Thy peace, Lord.

3 Peace in our hearts our evil thoughts
assuaging,
Peace in Thy church when disputes are
engaging,
Peace when the world its busy war is
waging,
Calm Thy foes' raging.

4 Grant us Thy help till backward they are
driven,
Grant them Thy truth, that they may be
forgiven,
Grant peace on earth, and after we have
striven,
Peace in Thy heaven.

485 © Timothy Dudley-Smith, b. 1926

1 **Lord of the church, we pray for our
renewing:**
Christ over all, our undivided aim;
Fire of the Spirit, burn for our enduing,
Wind of the Spirit, fan the living flame!
We turn to Christ amid our fear and failing,
The will that lacks the courage to be free,
The weary labours, all but unavailing,
To bring us nearer what a church should
be.

2 Lord of the church, we seek a Father's
blessing,
A true repentance and a faith restored,
A swift obedience and a new possessing,
Filled with the Holy Spirit of the Lord!
We turn to Christ from all our restless
striving,
Unnumbered voices with a single prayer –
The living water for our souls' reviving,
In Christ to live, and love and serve and
care.

3 Lord of the church, we long for our uniting,
True to one calling, by one vision stirred;
One cross proclaiming and one creed
reciting,
One in the truth of Jesus and His word!
So lead us on, till toil and trouble ended,
One church triumphant one new song shall
sing,
To praise His glory, risen and ascended,
Christ over all, the everlasting King!

486 Henry Williams Baker, 1821–77

1 **Lord, Thy Word abideth,**
And our footsteps guideth;
Who its truth believeth
Light and joy receiveth.

2 Who can tell the pleasure,
Who recount the treasure,
By Thy Word imparted
To the simple-hearted?

3 When the storms are o'er us,
And dark clouds before us,
Then its light directeth,
And our way protecteth.

4 When our foes are near us,
Then Thy Word doth cheer us,
Word of consolation,
Message of salvation.

5 Word of mercy, giving
  Succour to the living;
  Word of life, supplying
  Comfort to the dying.

6 O that we discerning
  Its most holy learning,
  Lord, may love and fear Thee,
  Evermore be near Thee!

487

**Lord, You are more precious than
  silver,**
Lord, You are more costly than gold.
Lord, You are more beautiful than
  diamonds,
And nothing I desire compares with You.

488
George Wade Robinson, 1838–77

1 **Loved with everlasting love,**
  Led by grace that love to know,
  Spirit, breathing from above,
  You have taught me it is so.
  O this full and perfect peace!
  O this presence so divine!
  In a love which cannot cease,
  I am His, and He is mine.

2 Heaven above is softer blue,
  Earth around is sweeter green;
  Something lives in every hue
  Christless eyes have never seen:
  Birds with gladder songs o'er-flow,
  Flowers with deeper beauties shine,
  Since I know, as now I know,
  I am His, and He is mine.

3 His for ever, only His;
  Who the Lord and me shall part?
  Ah, with what a rest of bliss
  Christ can fill the loving heart!
  Heaven and earth may fade and flee;
  First-born light in gloom decline;
  But while God and I shall be,
  I am His, and He is mine.

489
Christina Georgina Rossetti, 1830–94

1 **Love came down at Christmas,**
  Love all lovely, Love Divine;
  Love was born at Christmas,
  Star and angels gave the sign.

2 Worship we the God-head,
  Love Incarnate, Love Divine;
  Worship we our Jesus:
  But where-with for sacred sign?

3 Love shall be our token,
  Love be yours and love be mine,
  Love to God and all men,
  Love for plea and gift and sign.

490
Susie Hare

May the Lord bless you and keep you,
Make His face to shine upon you
And be gracious unto you.
May the Lord lift up the light
Of His countenance upon you
And give you peace.

491
Graham Kendrick

1 **Make way, make way, for Christ the
    King**
  In splendour arrives.
  Fling wide the gates and welcome Him
  Into your lives.

    Make way! Make way!
    For the King of kings.
    Make way! Make way!
    And let His kingdom in.

2 He comes the broken hearts to heal,
  The prisoners to free;
  The deaf shall hear, the lame shall dance,
  The blind shall see.
    Make way! . . .

3 And those who mourn with heavy hearts,
  Who weep and sigh,
  With laughter, joy and royal crown
  He'll beautify.
    Make way! . . .

4 We call You now to worship Him
  As Lord of all.
  To have no gods before Him,
  Their thrones must fall.
    Make way! . . .

492

Graham Kendrick
© 1986 Thankyou Music

1 **May the fragrance of Jesus
  fill this place,** *(men)*
  May the fragrance of Jesus
  fill this place, *(ladies)*
  May the fragrance of Jesus
  fill this place, *(men)*
  Lovely fragrance of Jesus *(ladies)*
  Rising from the sacrifice ⎤ *(all)*
  Of lives laid down in adoration. ⎦

2 May the glory of Jesus fill His church, *(men)*
  May the glory of Jesus
  fill His church, *(ladies)*
  May the glory of Jesus fill His church, *(men)*
  Radiant glory of Jesus *(ladies)*
  Shining from our faces ⎤ *(all)*
  As we gaze in adoration. ⎦

3 May the beauty of Jesus fill my life, *(men)*
  May the beauty of Jesus fill my life, *(ladies)*
  May the beauty of Jesus fill my life, *(men)*
  Perfect beauty of Jesus *(ladies)*
  Fill my thoughts, ⎤
  my words, my deeds, ⎥ *(all – twice)*
  My all I give in adoration. ⎦

493

Graham Kendrick
© 1986 Thankyou Music

1 **Meekness and majesty,**
  Manhood and Deity,
  In perfect harmony,
  The man who is God.
  Lord of eternity
  Dwells in humanity,
  Kneels in humility
  And washes our feet.

  Oh, what a mystery,
  Meekness and majesty,
  Bow down and worship,
  For this is your God,
  This is your God.

2 Father's pure radiance,
  Perfect in innocence,
  Yet learns obedience
  To death on a cross.
  Suffering to give us life,
  Conquering through sacrifice;
  And as they crucify
  Prays Father forgive.
  Oh, what a . . .

3 Wisdom unsearchable,
  God the invisible;
  Love indestructable
  In frailty appears.
  Lord of infinity
  Stooping so tenderly
  Lifts our humanity
  To the heights of His throne.
  Oh, what a . . .

494

Carolyn Govier
© 1979 Springtide / Word Music (UK)

My heart overflows with a goodly
theme,
I will address my verses to the King;
My heart overflows with praise to my God,
I'll give Him the love of my heart.

1 For He is Lord of all the earth, He's risen
    above,
  He's seated at God's right hand,
  And from Him and through Him and to Him
    are all things,
  That His glory might fill the land.
    My heart overflows . . .

2 For He has chosen Mount Zion as His resting
    place,
  He says, 'Here will I dwell,
  I will abundantly bless and satisfy,
  And her saints will shout for joy.
    My heart overflows . . .

3 'Lift up your eyes round about and see,
  Your heart shall thrill and rejoice,
  For the abundance of the nations is coming
    to you,
  I am glorifying My house.'
    My heart overflows . . .

495

© 1987 Ruth Hooke

My life is Yours, O Lord,
My life is Yours, O Lord,
So do as You will,
Do what is pleasing to You
For my life belongs to You.

Teach me the fear of the Lord,
Let me see Your righteousness.
I will kneel before You
And worship Christ my King.

496

Joan Parsons
© 1978 Thankyou Music

My Lord, He is the fairest of the fair,
He is the lily of the valley,
The bright and morning star,
His love is written deep within my heart,
He is the never ending fountain
Of everlasting life.
And He lives, He lives,
He lives, He lives in me.

497

Keith Routledge
© 1975 Kenwood Music

1 **My peace I give unto you,**
It's a peace that the world cannot give,
It's a peace that the world cannot
understand.
Peace to know, peace to live.
My peace I give unto you.

2 My joy I give unto you,
It's a joy that the world cannot give,
It's a joy that the world cannot understand.
Joy to know, joy to live.
My joy I give unto you.

3 My love I give unto you,
It's a love that the world cannot give,
It's a love that the world cannot understand.
Love to know, love to live.
My love I give unto you.

498

Frederick William Faber, 1814–63
Altered © 1987 Horrobin/Leavers

1 **My God, how wonderful You are,**
Your majesty how bright!
How beautiful Your mercy seat,
In depths of burning light!

2 In awe I glimpse eternity,
O everlasting Lord,
By angels worshipped day and night,
Incessantly adored!

3 O how I love You, Living God,
Who my heart's longing hears,
And worship You with certain hope,
And penitential tears!

4 Yes I may love You, O my Lord,
Almighty King of Kings,
For You have stooped to live in me,
With joy my heart now sings.

5 How wonderful, how beautiful,
Your loving face must be,
Your endless wisdom, boundless power,
And awesome purity!

499

© Timothy Dudley-Smith, b. 1926

1 **Name of all majesty,**
Fathomless mystery,
King of the ages
By angels adored;
    Power and authority,
    Splendour and dignity,
    Bow to His mastery –
Jesus is Lord!

2 Child of our destiny,
God from eternity,
Love of the Father
On sinners outpoured;
    See now what God has done
    Sending His only Son,
    Christ the belovèd One –
Jesus is Lord!

3 Saviour of Calvary,
Costliest victory,
Darkness defeated
And Eden restored –
    Born as a man to die,
    Nailed to a cross on high,
    Cold in the grave to lie –
Jesus is Lord!

4 Source of all sovereignty,
Light, immortality,
Life everlasting
And heaven assured;
    So with the ransomed, we
    Praise Him eternally,
    Christ in His majesty –
Jesus is Lord!

500

Tom Dowell
© 1982 Christian Fellowship of Columbia

No weapon formed, or army or king,
Shall be able to stand
Against the Lord and His Anointed.

All principalities and powers
Shall crumble before the Lord;
And men's hearts shall be released,
And they shall come unto the Lord.

No weapon form'd, or army or king,
Shall be able to stand
Against the Lord and His Anointed.

501

Johann Andreas Rothe, 1688–1758
tr. John Wesley, 1703–91
Altered © 1987 Horrobin/Leavers

1 **Now I have found the ground wherein**
Sure my soul's anchor may remain –
The wounds of Jesus, for my sin
Before the world's foundation slain;
Whose mercy shall unshaken stay,
When heaven and earth are fled away.

2 Father, Your everlasting grace
Our human thought surpassing far,
Your heart still melts with tenderness,
Your arms of love still open are
Returning sinners will receive,
Eternal life as they believe.

3 Your love, eternal hope, no less,
My sins consumed at Calvary!
Covered is my unrighteousness,
Nor spot of guilt remains on me,
While Jesu's blood through earth and skies
Mercy, free, boundless mercy! cries.

4 Though waves and storms go o'er my head,
Though strength, and health, and friends be
        gone,
Though joys be withered all and dead,
Though every comfort be withdrawn,
On this my steadfast soul relies—
Father, Your mercy never dies!

5 Fixed on this ground will I remain,
Though my heart fail and flesh decay;
This anchor shall my soul sustain,
When earth's foundations melt away:
Mercy's full power I then shall prove,
Loved with an everlasting love.

502

Sarah Flower Adams, 1805–48

1 **Nearer, my God to Thee,**
Nearer to Thee;
E'en though it be a cross
That raiseth me,
Still all my song would be
Nearer, my God to Thee,
Nearer to Thee, nearer to Thee.

2 Though, like the wanderer,
The sun gone down,
Darkness be over me,
My rest a stone,
Yet in my dreams I'd be
Nearer, my God to Thee,
Nearer to Thee, nearer to Thee.

3 There let the way appear,
Steps up to heaven;
All that Thou sendest me,
In mercy given;
Angels to beckon me
Nearer, my God to Thee,
Nearer to Thee, nearer to Thee.

4 Then, with my waking thoughts
Bright with Thy praise,
Out of my stony griefs
Bethel I'll raise;
So by my woes to be
Nearer, my God to Thee,
Nearer to Thee, nearer to Thee.

5 Or, if on joyful wing
Cleaving the sky,
Sun, moon, and stars forgot,
Upwards I fly,
Still all my song shall be,
Nearer, my God to Thee,
Nearer to Thee, nearer to Thee.

503

Isaac Watts, 1674–1748

1 **O God, our help in ages past,**
Our hope for years to come,
Our shelter from the stormy blast,
And our eternal home.

2 Under the shadow of Your throne
Your saints have dwelt secure;
Sufficient is Your arm alone,
And our defence is sure.

3 Before the hills in order stood,
Or earth received her frame,
From everlasting You are God,
To endless years the same.

4 A thousand ages in Your sight
Are like an evening gone,
Short as the watch that ends the night
Before the rising sun.

5 Time, like an ever-rolling stream,
Bears all its sons away;
They fly forgotten, as a dream
Dies with the dawning day.

6 O God, our help in ages past,
Our hope for years to come,
Be our defence while life shall last,
And our eternal home.

504

Latin, 18th century
tr. Frederick Oakley, 1802–80
Altered © 1986 Horrobin/Leavers

1 **O come, all you faithful,**
Joyful and triumphant,
O come now, O come now to Bethlehem;
Come and behold Him,
Born the King of angels:

> *O come, let us adore Him,*
> *O come, let us adore Him,*
> *O come, let us adore Him,*
> *Christ the Lord.*

2 True God of true God,
Light of light eternal,
He, who abhors not the virgin's womb;
Son of the Father,
Begotten not created:
O come, let us adore Him . . .

3 Sing like the angels,
Sing in exultation,
Sing with the citizens of heaven above,
'Glory to God,
Glory in the highest':
O come, let us adore Him . . .

ON CHRISTMAS DAY SING WORDS IN ITALICS
4 Yes, Lord, we greet You,
Born that *(this)* happy morning,
Jesus, to you be glory given;
Word of the Father,
Then *(Now)* in flesh appearing:
O come, let us adore Him . . .

505

Iain Anderson
© 1981 Springtide / Word Music (UK)

O come let us worship and bow down,
Let us kneel before the Lord our King.
Let us whisper His name, wonderful name,
Jesus our Lord and King.

For He is Lord of all the earth,
His glory outshines the sun.
See Him clothed in His robes of
righteousness,
God's beloved Son.
O come let us . . .

506

From Antiphons in 'Latin Breviary', 12th century
tr. John Mason Neale, 1818–66

1 **O come, O come, Emmanuel,**
And ransom captive Israel,
That mourns in lonely exile here
Until the Son of God appear.

> *Rejoice! Rejoice! Emmanuel*
> *Shall come to thee, O Israel.*

2 O come, O come, Thou Lord of might,
Who to Thy tribes, on Sinai's height,
In ancient times didst give the law
In cloud, and majesty, and awe.
Rejoice! Rejoice! . . .

3 O come, Thou Rod of Jesse, free
Thine own from Satan's tyranny;
From depths of hell Thy people save,
And give them victory o'er the grave.
Rejoice! Rejoice! . . .

4 O come, Thou Day-spring, come and cheer
Our spirits by Thine advent here;
Disperse the gloomy clouds of night,
And death's dark shadows put to flight.
Rejoice! Rejoice! . . .

5 O come, Thou Key of David, come,
And open wide our heavenly home;
Make safe the way that leads on high,
And close the path to misery.
Rejoice! Rejoice! . . .

507

Shona Sauni
© 1982 Scripture in Song / Thankyou Music

1 **O, I will sing unto You with joy, O
Lord,**
For You're the rock of my salvation,
Come before You with thanksgiving
And extol You with a song.

2 For You're the greatest King above all else,
You hold the depths of the earth in Your
hand.
O, I will sing unto You with joy, O Lord,
For You're the rock of my salvation.

508

John Wimber
© 1979 Mercy Music Publishing /
Word Music (UK)

1 **O let the Son of God enfold you**
With His Spirit and His love,
Let Him fill your heart and satisfy your soul.
O let Him have the things that hold you,
And His Spirit like a dove
Will descend upon your life and make you
whole.

> *Jesus, O Jesus,*
> *Come and fill Your lambs.*
> *Jesus, O Jesus,*
> *Come and fill Your lambs.*

2 O come and sing this song with gladness
As your hearts are filled with joy,
Lift your hands in sweet surrender to His
name.
O give Him all your tears and sadness,
Give Him all your years of pain,
And you'll enter into life in Jesus' name.
Jesus, O Jesus, . . .

509 Phillips Brooks, 1835–93

1 **O little town of Bethlehem,**
How still we see you lie!
Above your deep and dreamless sleep
The silent stars go by:
Yet in your dark streets shining
Is everlasting Light;
The hopes and fears of all the years
Are met in you tonight.

2 For Christ is born of Mary;
And, gathered all above
While mortals sleep, the angels keep
Their watch of wondering love.
O morning stars, together
Proclaim the holy birth,
And praises sing to God the King,
And peace to men on earth.

3 How silently, how silently,
The wondrous gift is given!
So God imparts to human hearts
The blessings of His heaven.
No ear may hear His coming;
But in this world of sin,
Where meek souls will receive Him, still
The dear Christ enters in.

4 O holy child of Bethlehem,
Descend to us, we pray;
Cast out our sin, and enter in;
Be born in us today.
We hear the Christmas angels
The great glad tidings tell;
O come to us, abide with us,
Our Lord Immanuel.

510 Carl Tuttle
© 1982 Mercy Publishing / Thankyou Music

1 **O Lord have mercy on me, and heal
me.**
O Lord have mercy on me, and free me.
Place my feet upon a rock,
Put a new song in my heart, in my heart,
O Lord have mercy on me.

2 O Lord may Your love and Your grace
protect me.
O Lord may Your ways and Your truth
direct me.
Place my feet upon a rock,
Put a new song in my heart, in my heart,
O Lord have mercy on me.

Place my feet upon a rock,
Put a new song in my heart, in my heart,
O Lord have mercy on me,
O Lord have mercy on me, on me.

511 Wendy Churchill
© 1980 Springtide / Word Music (UK)

1 **O Lord most Holy God,**
Great are Your purposes,
Great is Your will for us,
Great is Your love.
And we rejoice in You,
And we will sing to You,
O Father have Your way,
Your will be done.

2 For You are building
A temple without hands,
A city without walls
Enclosed by fire.
A place for You to dwell,
Built out of living stones,
Shaped by a Father's hand
And joined in love.

512 Phil Lawson Johnston
© 1982 Thankyou Music

1 **O Lord our God, how majestic is Your
name,**
The earth is filled with Your glory.
O Lord our God, You are robed in majesty,
You've set Your glory above the heavens.

We will magnify, we will magnify
The Lord enthroned in Zion.
We will magnify, we will magnify
The Lord enthroned in Zion.

2 O Lord our God, You have established a
throne,
You reign in righteousness and splendour.
O Lord our God, the skies are ringing with
Your praise,
Soon those on earth will come to worship.
We will magnify . . .

3 O Lord our God, the world was made at
     Your command,
   In You all things now hold together.
   Now to Him who sits on the throne and to
     the Lamb,
   Be praise and glory and power for ever.
   We will magnify . . .

513
Dave Fellingham
© 1983 Thankyou Music

O Lord, You are my light,
O Lord, You are my salvation.
You have delivered me from all my fear,
For You are the defence of my life.

For my life is hidden with Christ in God.
You have concealed me in Your love,
You've lifted me up, placed my feet on a
  rock.
I will shout for joy in the house of God.

514
Keith Green
© 1980 Birdwing Music / Cherry Lane Music Ltd.

1 **O Lord, You're beautiful,**
   Your face is all I seek,
   For When Your eyes are on this child,
   Your grace abounds to me.

2 O Lord, please light the fire
   That once burned bright and clear,
   Replace the lamp of my first love
   That burns with holy fear!

     *I want to take Your word and shine it all
       around,
     But first help me just to live it Lord!
     And when I'm doing well,
     help me to never seek a crown,
     For my reward is giving glory to You.*

3 O Lord You're beautiful,
   Your face is all I seek,
   For when Your eyes are on this child,
   Your grace abounds to me.

515
Horatius Bonar, 1808–89

1 **O love of God, how strong and true!**
   Eternal and yet ever new;
   Uncomprehended and unbought,
   Beyond all knowledge and all thought.

2 O heavenly love, how precious still,
   In days of weariness and ill,
   In nights of pain and helplessness,
   To heal, to comfort, and to bless!

3 O wide-embracing, wondrous love,
   We see You in the sky above;
   We see You in the earth below,
   In seas that swell and streams that flow.

4 We see You best in Him who came
   To bear for us the cross of shame,
   Sent by the Father from on high,
   Our life to live, our death to die.

5 We see Your power to bless and save
   E'en in the darkness of the grave;
   Still more in resurrection-light,
   We see the fulness of Your might.

6 O love of God, our shield and stay
   Through all the perils of our way;
   Eternal love, in You we rest,
   For ever safe, for ever blessed!

516
Carolyn Govier
© 1979 Springtide / Word Music (UK)

**O Lord, You've done great things, and I
  will praise You,**
I will extol You and magnify Your Name.
O Lord, You've done great things, and I will
  praise You,
I will extol You and magnify Your Name.

I will sing praises unto You and remember
  Your goodness,
My past is forgiven and now I have life,
You crown me with steadfast love and
  tender mercy,
I'll do Your will and bless You, O Lord.

517
Graham Kendrick
© 1986 Thankyou Music

O Lord, Your tenderness
Melting all my bitterness,
O Lord, I receive Your love,
O Lord, Your loveliness
Changing all my ugliness,
O Lord, I receive Your love,
O Lord, I receive Your love,
O Lord, I receive Your love.

518
William Walsham How, 1823–97

1 **O my Saviour, lifted**
From the earth for me,
Draw me, in Thy mercy,
Nearer unto Thee.

2 Lift my earth-bound longings,
Fix them, Lord above;
Draw me with the magnet
Of Thy mighty love.

3 And I come, Lord Jesus;
Dare I turn away?
No! Thy love hath conquered,
And I come today.

4 Bringing all my burdens,
Sorrow, sin, and care;
At Thy feet I lay them,
And I leave them there.

519
Henry Williams Baker, 1821–77

1 **O praise ye the Lord!**
Praise Him in the height;
Rejoice in His Word,
Ye angels of light;
Ye heavens adore Him
By Whom ye were made,
And worship before Him,
In brightness arrayed.

2 O praise ye the Lord!
Praise Him upon earth,
In tuneful accord,
Ye sons of new birth;
Praise Him Who has brought you
His grace from above,
Praise Him Who has taught you
To sing of His love.

3 O praise ye the Lord!
All things that give sound;
Each jubilant chord,
Re-echo around;
Loud organs, His glory
Forth tell in deep tone,
And sweet harp, the story
Of what He has done.

4 O praise ye the Lord!
Thanksgiving and song
To Him be outpoured
All ages along;
For love in creation,
For heaven restored,
For grace of salvation,
O praise ye the Lord!

520
Dorothy Frances Gurney, 1858–1932

1 **O perfect Love, all human thought**
transcending,
Lowly we kneel in prayer before Your
throne,
That theirs may be the love which knows no
ending,
Whom You for evermore now join as one.

2 O perfect Life, be now their full assurance
Of tender charity and steadfast faith,
Of patient hope, and quiet, brave
endurance,
With child-like trust that fears nor pain nor
death.

3 Grant them the joy which brightens earthly
sorrow,
Grant them the peace which calms all
earthly strife;
And to life's day the glorious unknown
morrow
That dawns upon eternal love and life.

521
Paulus Gerhardt, 1607–76
attributed to Bernard of Clairvaux, 1091–1153
tr. James Waddell Alexander, 1804–59

1 **O sacred Head once wounded,**
With grief and pain weighed down,
How scornfully surrounded
With thorns, Thine only crown!
How pale art Thou with anguish,
With sore abuse and scorn!
How does that visage languish
Which once was bright as morn!

2 O Lord of Life and Glory,
What bliss till now was Thine!
I read the wondrous story,
I joy to call Thee mine.
Thy grief and Thy compassion
Were all for sinners' gain;
Mine, mine was the transgression,
But Thine the deadly pain.

3 What language shall I borrow
To praise Thee, heavenly Friend,
For this Thy dying sorrow,
Thy pity without end?
Lord, make me Thine for ever,
Nor let me faithless prove;
O let me never, never
Abuse such dying love!

4 Be near me, Lord, when dying;
O show Thyself to me;
And, for my succour flying,
Come, Lord, to set me free:
These eyes, new faith receiving,
From Jesus shall not move;
For he who dies believing
Dies safely through Thy love.

522 Lucy Ann Bennett, 1850–1927

1 **O teach me what it meaneth,**
That cross uplifted high,
With One, the Man of Sorrows,
Condemned to bleed and die!
O teach me what it cost thee
To make a sinner whole;
And teach me, Saviour, teach me
The value of a soul!

2 O teach me what it meaneth,
That sacred crimson tide,
The blood and water flowing
From Thine own wounded side.
Teach me that if none other
Had sinned, but I alone,
Yet still Thy blood, Lord Jesus,
Thine only, must atone.

3 O teach me what it meaneth,
Thy love beyond compare,
The love that reacheth deeper
Than depths of self-despair!
Yes, teach me, till there gloweth
In this cold heart of mine
Some feeble, pale reflection
Of that pure love of thine.

4 O teach me what it meaneth,
For I am full of sin;
And grace alone can reach me,
And love alone can win.
O teach me, for I need Thee,
I have no hope beside,
The chief of all the sinners
For whom the Saviour died!

5 O Infinite Redeemer!
I bring no other plea,
Because Thou dost invite me
I cast myself on Thee.
Because Thou dost accept me
I love and I adore;
Because Thy love constraineth,
I'll praise Thee evermore!

523 Theodore Monod, 1836–1921
© in this version Jubilate Hymns

1 **O, the bitter shame and sorrow**
That a time could ever be
When I let the Saviour's pity
Plead in vain, and proudly answered,
'None of you and all of me.'

2 Yet You found me; there I saw You
Dying and in agony,
Heard You pray, 'Forgive them, Father',
And my wistful heart said faintly,
'Some of you and some of me.'

3 Day by day Your tender mercy,
Healing, helping, full and free,
Firm and strong, with endless patience
Brought me lower, while I whispered,
'More of You and less of me.'

4 Higher than the highest heaven,
Deeper than the deepest sea,
Lord, Your love at last has conquered:
Grant me now my spirit's longing,
'All of You and none of me!'

524 Henry Kirke White, 1785–1806
and others

1 **Oft in danger, oft in woe,**
Onward, Christians, onward go;
Bear the toil, maintain the strife,
Strengthened with the Bread of life.

2 Onward, Christians, onward go!
Join the war, and face the foe:
Will ye flee in danger's hour?
Know ye not your Captain's pow'r?

3 Let your drooping hearts be glad;
March in heav'nly armour clad;
Fight, nor think the battle long:
Vict'ry soon shall tune your song.

4 Let not sorrow dim your eye,
Soon shall every tear be dry;
Let not fears your course impede,
Great your strength, if great your need.

5 Onward then in battle move;
More than conquerors ye shall prove;
Though opposed by many a foe,
Christian soldiers, onward go.

525

Samuel Trevor Francis, 1834–1925

1 **O the deep, deep love of Jesus!**
Vast, unmeasured, boundless, free;
Rolling as a mighty ocean
In its fulness over me.
Underneath me, all around me,
Is the current of Thy love;
Leading onward, leading homeward,
To my glorious rest above.

2 O the deep, deep love of Jesus!
Spread His praise from shore to shore,
How He loveth, ever loveth,
Changeth never, nevermore;
How He watches o'er His loved ones,
Died to call them all His own;
How for them He intercedeth,
Watches over them from the throne.

3 O the deep, deep love of Jesus!
Love of every love the best:
'Tis an ocean vast of blessing,
'Tis a haven sweet of rest.
O the deep, deep love of Jesus!
'Tis a heaven of heavens to me;
And it lifts me up to glory,
For it lifts me up to Thee.

526

Dave Bilbrough
© 1980 Thankyou Music

O the valleys shall ring with the sound of praise,
And the lion shall lie with the lamb.
Of His government there shall be no end,
And His glory shall fill the earth.

May Your will be done, may Your kingdom come!
Let it rule, let it reign in our lives.
There's a shout in the camp as we answer the call,
Hail the King! Hail the Lord of lords!

527

Anon
Copyright control

Oh! Oh! Oh! how good is the Lord,
Oh! Oh! Oh! how good is the Lord,
Oh! Oh! Oh! how good is the Lord,
I never will forget what He has done for me.

1 He gives me salvation, how good is the Lord,
He gives me salvation, how good is the Lord,
He gives me salvation, how good is the Lord,
I never will forget what He has done for me.
Oh! Oh! Oh! . . .

2 He gives me His blessings . . .
Oh! Oh! Oh! . . .

3 He gives me His Spirit . . .
Oh! Oh! Oh! . . .

4 He gives me His healing . . .
Oh! Oh! Oh! . . .

5 He gives me His glory . . .
Oh! Oh! Oh! . . .

OTHER SUITABLE VERSES MAY BE ADDED
He gives us each other . . .
He gives us His body . . .
He gives us His freedom . . . *etc.*

528

Charles Coffin, 1676–1749,
tr. John Chandler, 1806–76, altd.,
Altered © 1986 Horrobin/Leavers

1 **On Jordan's bank the Baptist's cry**
Announces that the Lord is nigh;
Come then and listen for he brings
Glad tidings from the King of kings.

2 Then cleansed be every heart from sin;
Make straight the way for God within;
Prepare we in our hearts a home,
Where such a mighty guest may come.

3 For You are our salvation, Lord,
Our refuge and our great reward;
Without Your grace we waste away,
Like flowers that wither and decay.

4 To heal the sick stretch out Your hand,
Make wholeness flow at Your command;
Sin's devastation now restore
Earth's own true loveliness once more.

5 To Him who left the throne of heaven
To save mankind, all praise be given;
To God the Father, voices raise,
And Holy Spirit, let us praise.

529

Harriet Auber, 1773–1862

1 **Our blest Redeemer, ere He breathed**
His tender last farewell,
A Guide, a Comforter bequeathed,
With us to dwell.

2 He came in semblance of a dove,
With shelt'ring wings outspread,
The holy balm of peace and love
On earth to shed.

3 He came in tongues of living flame
To teach, convince, subdue;
All pow'rful as the wind He came
As viewless too.

4 He comes sweet influence to impart,
A gracious, willing Guest,
Where He can find one humble heart
Wherein to rest.

5 And His that gentle voice we hear,
Soft as the breath of even,
That checks each fault, that calms each fear,
And speaks of heaven.

6 For every virtue we possess,
And every victory won,
And every thought of holiness,
Are His alone.

7 Spirit of purity and grace,
Our weakness, pitying, see;
O make our hearts Thy dwelling-place,
And worthier Thee.

530

Cecil Frances Alexander, 1823–95
Altered © 1986 Horrobin/Leavers

1 **Once in royal David's city,**
Stood a lowly cattle shed,
Where a mother laid her Baby,
In a manger for His bed.
Mary was that mother mild,
Jesus Christ her little child.

2 He came down to earth from heaven,
Who is God and Lord of all,
And His shelter was a stable,
And His cradle was a stall:
With the poor and mean and lowly
Lived on earth our Saviour holy.

3 And through all His wondrous childhood
He would honour and obey,
Love and watch the lowly mother,
In whose gentle arms He lay.
Christian children all should be,
Kind, obedient, good as He.

4 For He is our childhood's pattern:
Day by day like us He grew;
He was little, weak, and helpless;
Tears and smiles like us He knew:
And He feels for all our sadness,
And He shares in all our gladness.

5 And our eyes at last shall see Him
Through His own redeeming love;
For that Child, so dear and gentle,
Is our Lord in heaven above;
And He leads His children on
To the place where He is gone.

6 Not in that poor, lowly stable,
With the oxen standing by,
We shall see Him, but in heaven,
Set at God's right hand on high;
There His children gather round
Bright like stars, with glory crowned.

531

Graham Kendrick
© 1981 Thankyou Music

1 **One shall tell another,**
And he shall tell his friend,
Husbands, wives and children
Shall come following on.
From house to house in families
Shall more be gathered in,
And lights will shine in ev'ry street,
So warm and welcoming.

Come on in and taste the new wine,
The wine of the kingdom,
The wine of the kingdom of God.
Here is healing and forgiveness,
The wine of the kingdom,
The wine of the kingdom of God.

2 Compassion of the Father
Is ready now to flow,
Through acts of love and mercy
We must let it show.
He turns now from His anger
To show a smiling face
And longs that men should stand beneath
The fountain of His grace.
Come on in . . .

3 He longs to do much more than
Our faith has yet allowed,
To thrill us and suprise us
With His sovereign power.
Where darkness has been darkest
The brightest light will shine,
His invitation comes to us,
It's yours and it is mine.
Come on in . . .

532

John Newton, 1725–1807

1 **One there is above all others**
Well deserves the name of Friend;
His is love beyond a brother's,
Costly, free, and knows no end:
They who once His kindness prove
Find it everlasting love.

2 Which of all our friends, to save us
Could, or would, have shed His blood?
Christ, the Saviour, died to have us
Reconciled in Him to God:
This was boundless love indeed!
Jesus is a Friend in need.

3 When He lived on earth abasèd,
'Friend of sinners' was His name;
Now above all glory raisèd
He rejoices in the same:
Still He calls them brethren, friends,
And to all their wants attends.

4 O for grace our hearts to soften!
Teach us, Lord, at length to love;
We, alas! forget too often
What a Friend we have above;
But when home our souls are brought,
We will love Thee as we ought.

533

Clara Scott, 1841–97

1 **Open my eyes that I may see**
Glimpses of truth Thou hast for me;
Place in my hands the wonderful key
That shall unclasp and set me free.

Silently now I wait for Thee,
Ready, my God, Thy will to see;
Open my eyes, illumine me,
Spirit Divine!

2 Open my ears that may hear
Voices of truth Thou sendest clear;
And while the wave-notes fall on my ear,
Ev'rything false will disappear.
Silently now . . .

3 Open my mouth and let me bear
Tidings of mercy ev'rywhere;
Open my heart and let me prepare
Love with Thy children thus to share.
Silently now . . .

4 Open my mind, that I may read
More of Thy love in word and deed:
What shall I fear while yet Thou dost lead?
Only for light from Thee I plead.
Silently now . . .

534

Our Father in heaven,
Hallowed be Your name,
Your kingdom come,
Your will be done,
On earth as in heaven.

Give us today our daily bread.
Forgive us our sins,
As we forgive those who sin against us.
Lead us not into temptation,
But deliver us from evil.

For the kingdom, the power and the glory
are Yours,
Now and for ever, Amen.
For the kingdom, the power and the glory
are Yours,
Now and for ever, Amen.

535

1 **Our eyes have seen the glory**
Of our Saviour, Christ the Lord;
He is seated at His Father's side
In love and full accord;
From there upon the sons of men
His Spirit is out-poured,
All hail, ascended King!

Glory, glory hallelujah,
Glory, glory hallelujah,
Glory, glory hallelujah,
All hail ascended King!

2 He came to earth at Christmas
And was made a man like us;
He taught, He healed, He suffered –
And they nailed Him to the cross;
He rose again on Easter Day –
Our Lord victorious,
All hail, ascended King!
Glory, glory . . .

3 The good news of His kingdom
Must be preached to every shore,
The news of peace and pardon,
And the end of strife and war;
The secret of His kingdom
Is to serve Him evermore,
All hail, ascended King!
Glory, glory . . .

4 His kingdom is a family
   Of men of every race,
   They live their lives in harmony,
   Enabled by His grace;
   They follow His example
   Till they see Him face to face,
   All hail, ascended King!
       Glory, glory . . .

536 W.T. Sleeper, 1840–1920

1 **Out of my bondage, sorrow, and night,**
   Jesus, I come: Jesus, I come.
   Into Your freedom, gladness, and light,
   Jesus, I come to You.
   Out of my sickness into Your health,
   Out of my want and into Your wealth,
   Out of my sin and into Yourself,
   Jesus, I come to You.

2 Out of my shameful failure and loss,
   Jesus, I come: Jesus, I come.
   Into the glorious gain of Your cross,
   Jesus, I come to You.
   Out of earth's sorrows into Your balm,
   Out of life's storm and into Your calm,
   Out of distress to jubilant psalm,
   Jesus, I come to You.

3 Out of unrest and arrogant pride,
   Jesus, I come: Jesus, I come.
   Into Your blessèd will to abide,
   Jesus, I come to You.
   Out of myself to dwell in Your love,
   Out of despair into joy from above,
   Upward for ever on wings like a dove,
   Jesus, I come to You.

4 Out of the fear and dread of the tomb,
   Jesus, I come: Jesus, I come.
   Into the joy and light of Your home,
   Jesus, I come to You.
   Out of the depths of ruin untold,
   Into the peace of Your sheltering fold,
   Ever Your glorious face to behold,
   Jesus, I come to You.

537

1 **Our Father who is in heaven,**
   Hallowed be Your Name,
   Your Kingdom come, Your will be done,
   Hallowed be Your Name.

2 On earth as it is in heaven,
   Hallowed be Your Name,
   Give us this day our daily bread,
   Hallowed be Your Name.

3 Forgive us all our trespasses,
   Hallowed be Your Name,
   As we forgive those who trespass against
       us,
   Hallowed be Your Name.

4 And lead us not into temptation,
   Hallowed be Your Name,
   But deliver us from all that is evil,
   Hallowed be Your Name.

5 For Yours is the Kingdom, the Power and
       the Glory,
   Hallowed be Your Name,
   For ever and for ever
   Hallowed be Your Name.

6 Amen, Amen, it shall be so,
   Hallowed be Your Name
   Amen, Amen, it shall be so,
   Hallowed be Your Name.

538 Graham Kendrick

1 **Peace, I give to you, I give to you My**
       peace.
   Peace, I give to you, I give to you My peace.

       Let it flow to one another, let it flow, let it
           flow.
       Let it flow to one another, let it flow, let it
           flow.

2 Love I give to you, I give you My love.
   Love I give to you, I give you My love.
       Let it flow . . .

3 Hope I give to you, I give you My hope.
   Hope I give to you, I give you My hope.
       Let it flow . . .

4 Joy I give to you, I give you My joy.
   Joy I give to you, I give you My joy.
       Let it flow . . .

539

John Kennett
© 1981 Thankyou Music

**Praise Him on the trumpet, the psaltery
and harp,**
Praise Him on the timbrel and the dance,
Praise Him with stringed instruments too.

Praise Him on the loud cymbals,
Praise Him on the loud cymbals,
Let ev'rything that has breath praise the
Lord.

Hallelujah, praise the Lord,
Hallelujah, praise the Lord,
Let ev'rything that has breath
praise the Lord. ⟧ repeat

540

David J. Hadden
© 1982 Restoration Music Ltd

Praise the Lord,
Praise God in His sanctuary,
Praise Him in His mighty heavens.
Praise Him for His greatness
And praise Him for His power.

1 Praise Him with the sound of trumpets,
Praise Him with the harp and lyre,
Praise Him with the tambourine and with
dancing.
Let everything that has breath praise the
Lord.
Praise the Lord . . .

2 Praise Him with the clash of cymbals,
Praise Him with the strings and flute,
Praise Him with the tambourine and with
dancing.
Let everything that has breath praise the
Lord.
Praise the Lord . . .

541

N. Rose
© 1977 Thankyou Music

1 **Praise You, Lord, for the wonder of Your
healing.**
Praise You, Lord, for Your love so freely
given,
Out-pouring, anointing, flowing in to heal
our wounds.
Praise You, Lord, for Your love for me.

2 Praise You, Lord, for Your gift of liberation.
Praise You, Lord, You have set the captives
free;
The chains that bind are broken by the
sharpness of Your sword,
Praise You, Lord, You gave Your life for
me.

3 Praise You, Lord, You have born the depths
of sorrow.
Praise You, Lord, for Your anguish on the
tree;
The nails that tore Your body and the pain
that tore Your soul.
Praise You, Lord, Your tears, they fell for
me.

4 Praise You, Lord, You have turned our
thorns to roses.
Glory, Lord, as they bloom upon Your
brow.
The path of pain is hallowed, for Your love
has made it sweet,
Praise You, Lord, and may I love You now.

542

Mike Kerry
© 1984 Thankyou Music

1 **Reconciled, I'm reconciled,**
I'm reconciled to God for ever,
Know He took away my sin,
I know His love will leave me never.
Reconciled, I am His child,
I know it was on me He smiled,
I'm reconciled, I'm reconciled to God,
Hallelujah.

2 I'm justified, I'm justified,
It's just as if I'd never sinned,
And once I knew such guilty fear,
But now I know His peace with me,
Justified, I'm justified,
It's all because my Jesus died,
I'm justified, I'm justified by God.
Hallelujah.

3 I'll magnify, I'll magnify,
I'll magnify His name for ever,
Wear the robe of righteousness
And bless the name of Jesus, Saviour,
Magnify the One who died,
The One who reigns for me on high.
I'll magnify, I'll magnify my God.

543

Graham Kendrick
© 1983 Thankyou Music

Rejoice! Rejoice! Christ is in you,
The hope of glory in our hearts.
He lives! He lives!
His breath is in you,
Arise a mighty army,
We arise.

1 Now is the time for us
   To march upon the land,
   Into our hands
   He will give the ground we claim.
   He rides in majesty
   To lead us into victory,
   The world shall see that
   Christ is Lord!
   Rejoice! . . .

2 God is at work in us
   His purpose to perform,
   Building a kingdom
   Of power not of words,
   Where things impossible
   By faith shall be made possible;
   Let's give the glory
   To Him now.
   Rejoice! . . .

3 Though we are weak, His grace
   Is everything we need;
   We're made of clay
   But this treasure is within.
   He turns our weakness
   Into His opportunities,
   So that the glory
   Goes to Him.
   Rejoice! . . .

544   Horatius Bonar, 1808–89

1 **Rejoice and be glad! the Redeemer has
   come:**
   Go, look on His cradle, His cross, and His
   tomb.

   *Sound His praises, tell the story of Him
   who was slain;
   Sound His praises, tell with gladness He
   now lives again.*

2 Rejoice and be glad! it is sunshine at last;
   The clouds have departed, the shadows are
   past.
   Sound His praises . . .

3 Rejoice and be glad! for the blood has been
   shed;
   Redemption is finished, the price has been
   paid.
   Sound His praises . . .

4 Rejoice and be glad! now the pardon is free;
   The just for the unjust has died on the tree.
   Sound His praises . . .

5 Rejoice and be glad! for the Lamb that was
   slain,
   O'er death is triumphant, and now lives
   again.
   Sound His praises . . .

6 Rejoice and be glad! for our King is on high;
   He pleads now for us on His throne in the
   sky.
   Sound His praises . . .

7 Rejoice and be glad! for He's coming again;
   He'll come in great glory, the Lamb that was
   slain.
   Sound His praises . . .

545   Moira Austin
   © 1986 M.C. & M.M. Austin

1 **Rejoice! The Lord is risen!**
   He is the King of glory
   Mighty Redeemer,
   He has made us His own:
   Rejoice! The Lord is risen!
   Opened, the gate of heaven
   Bow down before Him
   For He comes to claim His own!

   *Glory to the King of Kings!
   Glory to the Lord of Lords!
   Jesus, we proclaim
   That You are Lord enthroned in majesty!
   Glory to the King of Kings!
   Glory to the Lord of Lords!
   Jesus, You are reigning
   Now on high for evermore!*

2 Rejoice! The Lord is risen!
   We are His holy nation
   Ransomed, forgiven,
   Washed in His precious Blood:
   Rejoice! The Lord is risen!
   Worthy His new creation
   Perfect and spotless
   As the Lamb upon the throne.
   Glory to the King . . .

3 Rejoice! The Lord is risen!
   Blessing and honour give Him
   Wisdom, authority,
   Belong to His Name:
   Rejoice! The Lord is risen!
   Angels and saints adore Him
   Worship and praise Him,
   singing 'Jesus Christ is Lord!'
   Glory to the King . . .

546
Chris A. Bowater
© 1985 Springtide / Word Music (UK)

Reign in me, sovereign Lord, reign in me,
Reign in me, sovereign Lord, reign in me,
Captivate my heart, let Your kingdom come,
Establish there Your throne, let Your will be
done.

547
Henry Hart Milman, 1791–1868

1 **Ride on, ride on in majesty!**
Hark, all the tribes 'Hosanna!' cry!
O Saviour meek, pursue Your road,
With palms and scattered garments
strowed.

2 Ride on, ride on in majesty!
In lowly pomp ride on to die:
O Christ, Your triumphs now begin
O'er captive death and conquered sin.

3 Ride on, ride on in majesty!
The angel armies of the sky
Look down with sad and wond'ring eyes
To see th'approaching sacrifice.

4 Ride on, ride on in majesty!
Your last and fiercest strife is nigh:
The Father on His sapphire throne
Awaits His own anointed Son.

5 Ride on, ride on in majesty!
In lowly pomp ride on to die;
Bow Your meek head to mortal pain,
Then take, O God Your power, and reign.

548
Dougie Brown
© 1980 Thankyou Music

1 **River wash over me,**
Cleanse me and make me new.
Bathe me, refresh me and fill me anew,
River wash over me.

2 Spirit watch over me,
Lead me to Jesus' feet.
Cause me to worship and fill me anew,
Spirit watch over me.

3 Jesus rule over me,
Reign over all my heart.
Teach me to praise You and fill me anew,
Jesus rule over me.

549
© Timothy Dudley-Smith, b. 1926

1 **Safe in the shadow of the Lord**
Beneath His hand and power,
I trust in Him,
I trust in Him,
My fortress and my tower.

2 My hope is set on God alone
Though Satan spreads his snare;
I trust in Him,
I trust in Him
To keep me in His care.

3 From fears and phantoms of the night,
From foes about my way,
I trust in Him,
I trust in Him
By darkness as by day.

4 His holy angels keep my feet
Secure from every stone;
I trust in Him,
I trust in Him
And unafraid go on.

5 Strong in the everlasting name,
And in my Father's care,
I trust in Him,
I trust in Him
Who hears and answers prayer.

6 Safe in the shadow of the Lord,
Possessed by love divine,
I trust in Him,
I trust in Him
And meet His love with mine.

550
© 1986 Greg Leavers

*Saviour of the world, thank You for
dying on the cross.*
*All praise to You our risen Lord, Hallelujah!
Jesus.*

1 In the garden of Gethsemane Jesus knelt
and prayed,
For He knew the time was near when He
would be betrayed.
God gave Him the strength to cope with all
that people did to hurt Him;
Soldiers laughed and forced a crown of
thorns upon His head.
Saviour of the world, . . .

2 On a cross outside the city they nailed Jesus
   high;
   Innocent, but still He suffered as they
   watched Him die.
   Nothing that the soldiers did could make
   Him lose control, for Jesus
   Knew the time to die then 'It is finished', was
   His cry.
   Saviour of the world, . . .

3 Three days later by God's pow'r He rose
   up from the dead,
   For the tomb could not hold Jesus it was as
   He'd said;
   Victor over sin and death He conquered
   Satan's power; so let us
   Celebrate that Jesus is alive for ever more.
   Saviour of the world, . . .

551 Sylvanus Dryden Phelps, 1816–95

1 **Saviour! Thy dying love**
   Thou gavest me,
   Nor should I aught withhold,
   My Lord, from Thee;
   In love my soul would bow,
   My heart fulfil its vow,
   Some offering bring Thee now,
   Something for Thee.

2 At the blest mercy-seat,
   Pleading for me,
   My feeble faith looks up,
   Jesus, to Thee:
   Help me the cross to bear,
   Thy wondrous love declare,
   Some song to raise, or prayer,
   Something for Thee.

3 Give me a faithful heart,
   Likeness to Thee –
   That each departing day
   Henceforth may see
   Some work of love begun,
   Some deed of kindness done,
   Some wanderer sought and won,
   Something for Thee.

4 All that I am and have –
   Thy gifts so free –
   In joy, in grief, through life,
   O Lord, for Thee!
   And when Thy face I see
   My ransomed soul shall be
   Through all eternity
   Something for Thee.

552 Edward Caswell, 1814–78

1 **See, amid the winter's snow,**
   Born for us on earth below,
   See, the Lamb of God appears,
   Promised from eternal years.

   Hail thou ever blessèd morn!
   Hail, redemption's happy dawn!
   Sing through all Jerusalem:
   Christ is born in Bethlehem!

2 Lo, within a manger lies
   He Who built the starry skies,
   He Who, throned in height sublime,
   Sits amid the cherubim.
   Hail thou . . .

3 Say, ye holy shepherds, say,
   What your joyful news today;
   Wherefore have ye left your sheep
   On the lonely mountain steep?
   Hail thou . . .

4 As we watched at dead of night,
   Lo, we saw a wondrous light:
   Angels, singing peace on earth,
   Told us of the Saviour's birth.
   Hail thou . . .

5 Sacred Infant, all divine,
   What a tender love was Thine,
   Thus to come from highest bliss
   Down to such a world as this!
   Hail thou . . .

6 Teach, O teach us, holy Child,
   By Thy face so meek and mild,
   Teach us to resemble Thee
   In Thy sweet humility.
   Hail thou . . .

553 Michael Perry, b. 1942

1 **See Him lying on a bed of straw:**
   A draughty stable with an open door;
   Mary cradling the babe she bore—
   The Prince of glory is His name.

   O now carry me to Bethlehem
   To see the Lord appear to men!
   Just as poor as was the stable then,
   The Prince of glory when He came.

2 Star of silver, sweep across the skies,
   Show where Jesus in the manger lies;
   Shepherds swiftly from your stupor rise
   To see the Saviour of the world!
   O now carry . . .

3 Angels, sing the song that you began,
   Bring God's glory to the heart of man;
   Sing that Bethl'em's little baby can
   Be salvation to the soul.
   O now carry . . .

4 Mine are riches, from Your poverty,
   From Your innocence, eternity;
   Mine forgiveness by Your death for me,
   Child of sorrow for my joy.
   O now carry . . .

554 © 1987 Ruth Hooke

1 **See Him on the cross of shame**
   Dying for me,
   Bearing all my guilt and pain
   Dying for me.
   And how I love You
   Jesus my Redeemer,
   You gave Your life for me, O Lord,
   Now I give my life to You.

   Jesus lives, Jesus lives,
   Jesus lives in me.
   I will praise Your name.

2 They laid Him in a garden tomb,
   And sealed it with a stone.
   Mary wept her tears of grief –
   Her precious Lord had gone,
   'And how I love You,
   Jesus my Redeemer'
   Then she looked – the stone was rolled
        away –
   He had triumphed over death.
   Jesus lives . . .

555 H.E. Fox, 1841–1926

1 **Send forth the gospel! Let it run**
   Southward and northward, east and west:
   Tell all the earth Christ died and lives,
   He offers pardon, life, and rest.

2 Send forth Your gospel, mighty Lord!
   Out of the chaos bring to birth
   Your own creation's promised hope;
   The better days of heaven on earth.

3 Send forth Your gospel, gracious Lord!
   Yours was the blood for sinners shed;
   Your voice still pleads in human hearts;
   To You may all Your sheep be led.

4 Send forth Your gospel, holy Lord!
   Kindle in us love's sacred flame;
   Love giving all and grudging naught
   For Jesus' sake, in Jesus' name.

5 Send forth the gospel! Tell it out!
   Go, brothers, at the Master's call;
   Prepare His way, who comes to reign
   The King of kings and Lord of all.

556 John Pantry
   © Ears & Eyes Music

Send me out from here, Lord,
To serve a world in need,
May I know no man by the coat he wears,
But the heart that Jesus sees.

And may the light of Your face
Shine upon me Lord,
You have filled my heart with the greatest
     joy
and my cup is overflowing.

1 Go now and carry the news to all creation
   Every race and every tongue.
   Take no purse with you, take nothing to eat,
   For He will supply your every need.
   Send me out . . .

2 Go now bearing the light living for other's,
   Fearlessly walking into the night.
   Take no thought for your lives, like lambs
        among wolves,
   Full of the Spirit ready to die.
   Send me out . . .

557 Author unknown
   Copyright control

Set my spirit free that I might worship
   You,
Set my spirit free that I might praise Your
   name.
Let all bondage go and let deliverance flow,
Set my spirit free to worship You.

558 J. Mohr, d. 1848
   tr. S.A. Brooke, d. 1916

1 **Silent night, holy night!**
   Sleeps the world; hid from sight,
   Mary and Joseph in stable bare
   Watched o'er the Child beloved and fair
   Sleeping in heavenly rest,
   Sleeping in heavenly rest.

2 Silent night, holy night!
   Shepherds first saw the light;
   Heard resounding clear and long,
   Far and near, the angel song:
   'Christ the Redeemer is here,
   Christ the Redeemer is here.'

3 Silent night, holy night!
   Son of God, O how bright
   Love is smiling from Your face!
   Strikes for us now the hour of grace,
   Saviour, since You are born,
   Saviour, since You are born.

559 Frederick William Faber, 1814–63

1 **Souls of men, why will ye scatter**
   Like a crowd of frightened sheep?
   Foolish hearts, why will ye wander
   From a love so true and deep?

2 Was there ever kindest shepherd
   Half so gentle, half so sweet,
   As the Saviour Who would have us
   Come and gather round His feet?

3 There's a wideness in God's mercy
   Like the wideness of the sea;
   There's a kindness in His justice,
   Which is more than liberty.

4 There is plentiful redemption
   In the blood that has been shed;
   There is joy for all the members
   In the sorrows of the Head.

5 For the love of God is broader
   Than the measures of man's mind;
   And the heart of the Eternal
   Is most wonderfully kind.

6 If our love were but more simple,
   We should take Him at His word,
   And our lives would be all sunshine
   In the sweetness of our Lord.

560 from Psalm 98
© Michael Baughen, b. 1930

1 **Sing to God new songs of worship—**
   All His deeds are marvellous;
   He has brought salvation to us
   With His hand and holy arm:
   He has shown to all the nations
   Righteousness and saving power;
   He recalled His truth and mercy
   To His people Israel.

2 Sing to God new songs of worship—
   Earth has seen His victory;
   Let the lands of earth be joyful
   Praising Him with thankfulness:
   Sound upon the harp His praises,
   Play to Him with melody;
   Let the trumpets sound His triumph,
   Show your joy to God the king!

3 Sing to God new songs of worship—
   Let the sea now make a noise;
   All on earth and in the waters
   Sound your praises to the Lord:
   Let the hills be joyful together,
   Let the rivers clap their hands,
   For with righteousness and justice
   He will come to judge the earth.

561 Dave Bilbrough
© 1983 Thankyou Music

1 **So freely,**
   Flows the endless love You give to me;
   So freely,
   Not dependent on my part.
   As I am reaching out
   Reveal the love within Your heart,
   As I am reaching out
   Reveal the love within Your heart.

2 Completely,
   That's the way You give Your love to me,
   Completely,
   Not dependent on my part.
   As I am reaching out
   Reveal the love within Your heart,
   As I am reaching out
   Reveal the love within Your heart.

3 So easy,
   I receive the love You give to me.
   So easy,
   Not dependent on my part.
   Flowing out to me
   The love within Your heart,
   Flowing out to me
   The love within Your heart.

562 E. May Grimes 1868–1927

1 **Speak, Lord, in the stillness,**
   While I wait on Thee;
   Hushed my heart to listen
   In expectancy.

2 Speak, O blessèd Master,
In this quiet hour;
Let me see Thy face, Lord,
Feel Thy touch of power.

3 For the words Thou speakest,
'They are life' indeed;
Living Bread from heaven,
Now my spirit feed!

4 All to Thee is yielded,
I am not my own;
Blissful, glad surrender—
I am Thine alone.

5 Speak, Thy servant heareth!
Be not silent, Lord;
Waits my soul upon Thee
For the quickening word!

6 Fill me with the knowledge
Of Thy glorious will;
All Thine own good pleasure
In Thy child fulfil.

563 Andrew Reed, 1787–1862

1 **Spirit Divine, attend our prayers**
And make this house Thy home;
Descend with all Thy gracious powers,
O come, great Spirit, come!

2 Come as the Light: to us reveal
Our emptiness and woe;
And lead us in those paths of life
Where all the righteous go.

3 Come as the Fire, and purge our hearts
Like sacrificial flame;
Let our whole soul an offering be
To our Redeemer's name.

4 Come as the Dove, and spread Thy wings,
The wings of perfect love;
And let Thy church on earth become
Blest as the church above.

5 Spirit Divine, attend our prayers;
Make a lost world Thy home;
Descend with all Thy gracious powers,
O come, great Spirit, come!

564 © 1984 Colin Preston

1 **Spirit of God Divine**
Fill this heart of mine
With holy flame
To praise the name
Of Jesus my Lord.

Fill me again,
Fill me again,
Fill me again
O Spirit of the Lord.

2 Spirit of God Divine,
Fill this mouth of mine
With holy praise
To set the earth ablaze
And glorify Your name.
Fill me again . . .

3 Spirit of God Divine,
Take this heart of mine
To Your throne this day,
Help me I pray
My offering to give.
Fill me again . . .

565 © Christopher Idle, b. 1938

Spirit of holiness, wisdom and
faithfulness,
Wind of the Lord, blowing strongly and
free:
Strength of our serving and joy of our
worshipping –
Spirit of God, bring Your fulness to me!

1 You came to interpret and teach us
effectively
All that the Saviour has spoken and done;
To glorify Jesus is all Your activity –
Promise and gift of the Father and Son:
Spirit of holiness . . .

2 You came with Your gifts to supply all our
poverty,
Pouring Your love on the church in her
need;
You came with Your fruit for our growth to
maturity,
Richly refreshing the souls that You feed:
Spirit of holiness . . .

566
© 1986 Andy Silver

Stand up and bless the Lord your God,
Stand up and bless the Lord.
His name is exalted above all names,
Stand up and bless the Lord.

For our God is good to us,
Always ready to forgive,
He is gracious and merciful,
Slow to anger and very kind.

So, stand up and bless the Lord your God,
Stand up and bless the Lord.
Stand up and bless the Lord your God,
Stand up.

567
John Keble, 1792–1866

1 **Sun of my soul, My Saviour dear,**
It is not night if You are near;
O may no earth-born cloud arise
To hide You from Your servant's eyes.

2 When the soft dews of kindly sleep
My wearied eyelids gently steep,
Be my last thought, how sweet to rest
For ever on my Saviour's breast!

3 Abide with me from morn till eve,
For without You I cannot live;
Abide with me when night is nigh,
For without You I dare not die.

4 If some poor wandering child of Yours
Have spurned today Your holy voice,
Now, Lord, the gracious work begin;
Let them no more be ruled by sin.

5 Watch by the sick; enrich the poor
With blessings from Your boundless store;
Be every mourner's sleep tonight
Like infant's slumbers, pure and light.

6 Come near and bless us when we wake,
Ere through the world our way we take;
Till in the ocean of Your love
We lose ourselves in heaven above.

568
Isaac Watts, 1674–1748

1 **Sweet is the work, my God, my King,**
To praise Thy name, give thanks and sing;
To show Thy love by morning light,
And talk of all Thy truth at night.

2 Sweet is the day of sacred rest,
No mortal cares disturb my breast;
O may my heart in tune be found,
Like David's harp of solemn sound.

3 My heart shall triumph in the Lord,
And bless His works, and bless His word;
Thy works of grace, how bright they shine,
How deep Thy counsels, how divine!

4 And I shall share a glorious part,
When grace has well refined my heart,
And fresh supplies of joy are shed,
Like holy oil, to cheer my head.

5 Then shall I see, and hear, and know
All I desired or wished below;
And every power find sweet employ
In that eternal world of joy.

569
B. Mansell Ramsey, 1849–1923

1 **Teach me Thy way, O Lord,**
Teach me Thy way!
Thy gracious aid afford,
Teach me Thy way!
Help me to walk aright,
More by faith, less by sight;
Lead me with heav'nly light:
Teach me Thy way!

2 When doubts and fears arise,
Teach me Thy way!
When storms o'erspread the skies,
Teach me Thy way!
Shine through the cloud and rain,
Through sorrow, toil, and pain;
Make Thou my pathway plain:
Teach me Thy way!

3 Long as my life shall last,
Teach me Thy way!
Where'er my lot be cast,
Teach me Thy way!
Until the race is run,
Until the journey's done,
Until the crown is won,
Teach me Thy way!

570
Paul Simmons
© 1985 Thankyou Music

Take, eat, this is My body,
Broken for you,
For I am come that you might have life;
Eat of My flesh and live,
Eat of My flesh and live.

1 My blood was shed for many,
  Taking away your sin,
  And if I shall make you free then
  You shall be free indeed,
  You shall be free indeed.
    Take, eat, . . .

2 Though your sins be as scarlet
  They shall be white as snow,
  Though they be red like crimson
  They shall be as wool,
  They shall be as wool.
    Take, eat, . . .

3 For God so loved the world
  He gave His only Son,
  That whosoever believeth on Him
  Might have everlasting life,
  Might have everlasting life.
    Take, eat, . . .

3 Tell me the story softly,
  With earnest tones and grave;
  Remember! I'm the sinner
  Whom Jesus came to save.
  Tell me the story always,
  If you would really be,
  In any time of trouble,
  A comforter to me.
    Tell me the old, . . .

4 Tell me the same old story,
  When you have cause to fear
  That this world's empty glory
  Is costing me too dear.
  Yes, and when that world's glory
  Is dawning on my soul,
  Tell me the old, old story;
  'Christ Jesus makes you whole.'
    Tell me the old, . . .

571

Thank You, God, for sending Jesus;
Thank You, Jesus, that You came;
Holy Spirit, won't You teach us
More about His wondrous name?

572 Arabella C. Hankey, 1834–1911, altd.

1 **Tell me the old, old story**
  Of unseen things above,
  Of Jesus and His glory,
  Of Jesus and His love.
  Tell me the story simply,
  As to a little child,
  For I am weak and weary,
  And helpless and defiled.

    Tell me the old, old story,
    Tell me the old, old story,
    Tell me the old, old story,
    Of Jesus and His love.

2 Tell me the story slowly,
  That I may take it in—
  That wonderful redemption,
  God's remedy for sin.
  Tell me the story often,
  For I forget so soon:
  The early dew of morning
  Has passed away at noon.
    Tell me the old, . . .

573 W.H. Parker, 1845–1929, altd.
v.6 by Hugh Martin, 1890–
Altered © 1986 Horrobin/Leavers

1 **Tell me the stories of Jesus**
  I love to hear;
  Things I would ask Him to tell me
  If He were here;
  Scenes by the wayside,
  Tales of the sea,
  Stories of Jesus,
  Tell them to me.

2 First let me hear how the children
  Stood round His knee;
  That I may know of His blessing
  Resting on me;
  Words full of kindness,
  Deeds full of grace,
  Signs of the love found
  In Jesus' face.

3 Tell me in words full of wonder,
  How rolled the sea,
  Tossing the boat in a tempest
  On Galilee.
  Jesus then doing
  His Father's will,
  Ended the storm say'ng
  'Peace, peace be still.'

4 Into the city I'd follow
  The children's band,
  Waving a branch of the palm-tree
  High in my hand;
  Worshipping Jesus,
  Yes, I would sing
  Loudest Hosannas,
  For He is King.

5 Show me that scene in the garden,
  Of bitter pain;
  And of the cross where my Saviour
  For me was slain;
  And, through the sadness,
  Help me to see
  How Jesus suffered
  For love of me.

6 Gladly I'd hear of His rising
  Out of the grave,
  Living and strong and triumphant,
  Mighty to save;
  And how He sends us
  All men to bring
  Stories of Jesus,
  Jesus, their King.

574
Leonard Bartlotti
© 1975 Celebration / Thankyou Music

Tell my people I love them,
Tell my people I care.
When they feel far away from me,
Tell my people I am there.

1 Tell my people I came and died
  To give them liberty,
  And to abide in me
  Is to be really free.
    Tell my people . . .

2 Tell my people where'er they go
  My comfort they can know.
  My peace and joy and love
  I freely will bestow.
    Tell my people . . .

575
© 1987 Greg Leavers

SELECT VERSES AS APPROPRIATE

 1 **Thank You Lord, Thank You Lord**
   That nothing can separate us from Your
   love.

 2 Thank You Lord, Thank You Lord
   That there is no condemnation when we're
   in You.

CONFESSION VERSES
 3 Search my heart, Search my heart
   And show me the sin I need to confess to
   You.

 4 Sorry Lord, Sorry Lord,
   I humbly now ask forgiveness for my sin.

 5 Cleanse me Lord, Cleanse me Lord
   Through Your precious blood make my
     heart clean before You.

 6 Thank You Lord, Thank You Lord
   That You've now removed the guilt of all my
   sin.

COMMUNION
 7 Take this bread, Take this bread,
   For this is Christ's body which was broken
     for you.

 8 Thank You Lord, Thank You Lord
   For dying on Calv'ry so that I can know You.

 9 Take this cup, Take this cup
   And drink it rememb'ring Jesus Christ died
     for you.

10 Thank You Lord, Thank You Lord,
   That through Your shed blood we are made
   one with God.

PRAISE AND WORSHIP
11 Fill me Lord, Fill me Lord,
   So that I might learn to live through Your
     power alone.

12 We love You, We love You,
   We open our hearts in adoration to You.

13 Holy Lord, Holy Lord,
   Your Name is far higher than any other
     name.

14 Worthy Lord, Worthy Lord,
   We offer our sacrifice of worship to You.

15 Reigning King, Reigning King,
   You're glorious in Majesty, almighty in
     power.

576
Roland Fudge
© 1986 Ears & Eyes Music

1 **Thank You, Lord, for Your presence
    here,**
  Thank You Lord, thank You Lord.
  Thank You Lord, You remove all fear,
  Thank You Lord, thank You Lord.

2 For the love that You showed
As You poured out Your life,
We thank You, we bless You,
Christ Jesus our Lord,
We thank You, Lord.
Thank You, Lord.

577
Robert Stoodley
© 1978 Mustard Seed Music

Thanks be to God
Who gives us the victory,
Gives us the victory,
Through our Lord Jesus Christ.

1 He is able to keep us from falling
And to set us free from sin.
So let us each live up to our calling
And commit our way to Him.
Thanks be to God . . .

2 Jesus knows all about our temptations,
He has had to bear them too;
He will show us how to escape them
If we trust Him He will lead us through:
Thanks be to God . . .

3 He has led us from the power of darkness
To the kingdom of His blessed Son;
So let us join in praise together
And rejoice in what the Lord has done.
Thanks be to God . . .

4 Praise the Lord for sending Jesus
To the cross of Calvary:
Now He's risen, reigns in power
And death is swallowed up in victory.
Thanks be to God . . .

578
Alison Huntley
© 1978 Thankyou Music

Thank You, Jesus, for Your love to me.
Thank You, Jesus, for Your grace so free.
I'll lift my voice to praise Your name,
Praise You again and again.
You are everything,
You are my Lord.

579
Jamie Owens-Collins
© 1984 Fairhill Music / Word Music (UK)

1 **In heavenly armour we'll enter the
land,**
The battle belongs to the Lord.
No weapon that's fashioned against us will
stand,
The battle belongs to the Lord.

*We sing glory, honour, power and
strength to the Lord!*
*We sing glory, honour, power and
strength to the Lord!*

2 When the power of darkness comes in like a
flood,
The battle belongs to the Lord.
He's raised up a standard, the power of His
blood,
The battle belongs to the Lord.
We sing glory . . .

3 When your enemy presses in hard, do not
fear,
The battle belongs to the Lord.
Take courage, my friend, your redemption
is near,
The battle belongs to the Lord.
We sing glory . . .

580
Author unknown (c. 17th cent.)
© in this version Jubilate Hymns

1 **The first nowell the angel did say**
Was to Bethlehem's shepherds in fields as
they lay;
In fields where they lay keeping their sheep
On a cold winter's night that was so deep:

Nowell, nowell, nowell, nowell,
Born is the king of Israel!

2 Then wise men from a country far
Looked up and saw a guiding star;
They travelled on by night and day
To reach the place where Jesus lay:
Nowell, nowell . . .

3 At Bethlehem they entered in,
On bended knee they worshipped Him;
They offered there in His presence
Their gold and myrrh and frankincense:
Nowell, nowell . . .

4 Then let us all with one accord
Sing praises to our heavenly Lord;
For Christ has our salvation wrought
And with His blood mankind has bought:
Nowell, nowell . . .

581

Thomas Olivers, 1725–99, altd.

1 **The God of Abraham praise,**
Who reigns enthroned above,
Ancient of everlasting days,
And God of love.
Jehovah, great I AM!
By earth and heaven confessed;
We bow and bless the sacred name,
For ever blessed.

2 The God of Abraham praise,
At whose supreme command
From earth we rise, and seek the joys
At His right hand;
We all on earth forsake,
Its wisdom, fame, and power;
And Him our only portion make,
Our shield and tower.

3 The God of Abraham praise,
Whose all-sufficient grace
Shall guide us all our happy days,
In all our ways:
He is our faithful friend;
He is our gracious God;
And He will save us to the end,
Through Jesus' blood.

4 He by Himself has sworn—
We on His oath depend—
We shall, on eagles' wings upborne,
To heaven ascend:
We shall behold His face,
We shall His power adore,
And sing the wonders of His grace
For evermore.

5 The whole triumphant host
Give thanks to God on high:
'Hail, Father, Son, and Holy Ghost!'
They ever cry.
Hail, Abraham's God and ours!
We join the heavenly lays;
And celebrate with all our powers
His endless praise.

582

Bryn Rees, 1911–1983
© M.E. Rees

1 **The kingdom of God is justice and joy;**
For Jesus restores what sin would destroy.
God's power and glory in Jesus we know;
And here and hereafter the kingdom shall
grow.

2 The kingdom of God is mercy and grace;
The captives are freed, the sinners find
place,
The outcast are welcomed God's banquet to
share;
And hope is awakened in place of despair.

3 The kingdom of God is challenge and
choice:
Believe the good news, repent and rejoice!
His love for us sinners brought Christ to His
cross:
Our crisis of judgement for gain or for loss.

4 God's kingdom is come, the gift and the
goal;
In Jesus begun, in heaven made whole.
The heirs of the kingdom shall answer His
call;
And all things cry 'Glory!' to God all in all.

583

Anon
Copyright control

1 **The Lord has given a land of good
things,**
I will press on and make them mine.
I'll know His power I'll know His glory,
And in His kingdom I will shine.

*With the high praises of God in our mouth
And a two-edged sword in our hand,
We'll march right on to the victory side,
Right into Canaan's land.*

2 Gird up your armour, ye sons of Zion,
Gird up your armour, let's go to war.
We'll win the battle with great rejoicing
And so we'll praise Him more and more.
With the high praises . . .

3 We'll bind their kings in chains and fetters,
We'll bind their nobles tight in iron,
To execute God's written judgement.
March on to glory, sons of Zion!
With the high praises . . .

584

Angela Pack
© 1979 Springtide / Word Music (UK)

***The Lord reigns, the Lord reigns,**
He is robed in majesty,
The Lord is robed in majesty,
And He is girded with strength.*

1 The Lord has established the world,
It shall never be moved,
Thy throne is established of old,
Thou art from everlasting.
The Lord reigns, . . .

2 The floods have lifted up, O Lord,
Lifted up their voice,
Mightier than the thunder of the waves,
The Lord on high is mighty.
The Lord reigns, . . .

585 tr. from the Latin
by Francis Pott, 1832–1909

1 **The strife is o'er, the battle done;**
The victory of life is won;
The song of triumph has begun:
Hallelujah!

2 The powers of death have done their worst,
But Christ their legions has dispersed;
Let shouts of holy joy outburst:
Hallelujah!

3 The three sad days have quickly sped:
He rises glorious from the dead;
All glory to our risen Head:
Hallelujah!

4 He broke the bonds of death and hell;
The bars from heaven's high portals fell;
Let hymns of praise His triumphs tell:
Hallelujah!

5 Lord, by the stripes which wounded Thee,
From death's dread sting Thy servants free,
That we may live, and sing to Thee;
Hallelujah!

586 The Lord's Prayer

Our Father which art in heaven,
Hallowed be Thy name,
Thy kingdom come,
Thy will be done,
In earth, as it is in heaven.
Give us this day our daily bread.

Forgive us our trespasses
As we forgive them who trespass against us.
And lead us not into temptation,
But deliver us from evil.
For Thine is the kingdom, the power and
the glory
For ever and ever. Amen, Amen.

587 Graham Kendrick
© 1983 Thankyou Music

1 **The price is paid,**
Come let us enter in
To all that Jesus died
To make our own.
For ev'ry sin
More than enough He gave,
And bought our freedom
From each guilty stain.

The price is paid,
Alleluia,
Amazing grace,
So strong and sure.
And so with all my heart,
My life in ev'ry part,
I live to thank You
For the price You paid.

2 The price is paid,
See Satan flee away;
For Jesus crucified
Destroys his power.
No more to pay,
Let accusation cease,
In Christ there is
No condemnation now.
The price is paid, . . .

3 The price is paid,
And by that scourging cruel
He took our sickness
As if His own.
And by His wounds
His body broken there,
His healing touch may now
By faith be known.
The price is paid, . . .

4 The price is paid,
'Worthy the Lamb' we cry,
Eternity shall never
Cease His praise.
The Church of Christ
Shall rule upon the earth,
In Jesus' name we have
Authority.
The price is paid, . . .

588 Damian Lundy
Copyright control

1 **The Spirit lives to set us free,**
Walk, walk in the light.
He binds us all in unity,
Walk, walk in the light.

Walk in the light,
Walk in the light,
Walk in the light,
Walk in the light of the Lord.

2 Jesus promised life to all,
Walk, walk in the light.
The dead were wakened by His call,
Walk, walk in the light.
Walk in the light . . .

3 He died in pain on Calvary,
Walk, walk in the light.
To save the lost like you and me,
Walk, walk in the light.
Walk in the light . . .

4 We know His death was not the end,
Walk, walk in the light.
He gave His Spirit to be our friend,
Walk, walk in the light.
Walk in the light . . .

5 By Jesus' love our wounds are healed,
Walk, walk in the light.
The Father's kindness is revealed,
Walk, walk in the light.
Walk in the light . . .

6 The Spirit lives in you and me,
Walk, walk in the light.
His light will shine for all to see,
Walk, walk in the light.
Walk in the light . . .

589 © Chris Idle, b. 1938

1 **Then I saw a new heaven and earth**
For the first had passed away,
And the holy city, come down from God,
Like a bride on her wedding day.
And I know how He loves His own
For I heard His great voice tell
They would be His people, and He their
     God,
And among them He came to dwell.

2 He will wipe away every tear,
Even death shall die at last;
There'll be no more crying, or grief, or
     pain,
They belong to the world that's past.
And the One on the throne said 'Look!
I am making all things new';
He is A and Z, He is first and last,
And His words are exact and true.

3 So the thirsty can drink their fill
At the fountain giving life;
But the gates are shut on all evil things,
On deceit and decay and strife.
With foundations and walls and towers
Like a jewel the city shines,
With its streets of gold and its gates of pearl
In a glory where each combines.

4 As they measured its length and breadth
I could see no temple there,
For its only temple is God the Lord
And the Lamb in that city fair.
And it needs neither sun nor moon
In a place which knows no night,
For the city's lamp is the Lamb Himself
And the glory of God its light.

5 And I saw by the sacred throne
Flowing water, crystal clear,
And the tree of life with its healing leaves
And its fruit growing all the year.
So the worshippers of the Lamb
Bear His Name, and see His face;
And they reign and serve and for ever live
To the praise of His glorious grace.

590 Melody Green
© Cherry Lane Music Ltd

1 **There is a Redeemer,**
Jesus, God's own Son,
Precious Lamb of God,
Messiah, Holy One.

Thank You, O my Father,
For giving us Your Son,
And leaving Your Spirit
Till the work on earth is done.

2 Jesus my Redeemer,
Name above all names,
Precious Lamb of God, Messiah,
O for sinners slain.
Thank You . . .

3 When I stand in glory
I will see His face.
And there I'll serve my King for ever,
In that Holy Place.
Thank You . . .

591

W.E. Littlewood, 1831–86

1 **There is no love like the love of Jesus,**
Never to fade or fall,
Till into the fold of the peace of God
He has gathered us all.

Jesus' love, precious love,
Boundless and pure and free!
O turn to that love, weary wandering
soul,
Jesus pleadeth with thee.

2 There is no heart like the heart of Jesus,
Filled with a tender love,
No throb nor throe that our hearts can know
But He feels it above.
Jesus' love, . . .

3 O let us hark to the voice of Jesus!
O may we never roam,
Till safe we rest on His loving breast
In the dear heavenly home.
Jesus' love, . . .

592

Henry Burton, 1840–1930

1 **There's a light upon the mountains, and**
the day is at the spring,
When our eyes shall see the beauty and the
glory of the King;
Weary was our heart with waiting, and the
night-watch seemed so long;
But His triumph-day is breaking, and we hail
it with a song.

2 In the fading of the starlight we can see the
coming morn;
And the lights of men are paling in the
splendours of the dawn:
For the eastern skies are glowing as with
light of hidden fire,
And the hearts of men are stirring with the
throbs of deep desire.

3 There's a hush of expectation, and a quiet in
the air;
And the breath of God is moving in the
fervent breath of prayer:
For the suffering, dying Jesus is the Christ
upon the throne,
And the travail of our spirit is the travail of
His own.

4 He is breaking down the barriers, He is
casting up the way;
He is calling for His angels to build up the
gates of day:
But His angels here are human, not the
shining hosts above;
For the drum-beats of His army are the
heart-beats of our love.

5 Hark! we hear a distant music, and it comes
with fuller swell;
'Tis the triumph-song of Jesus, of our King,
Immanuel:
Zion, go ye forth to meet Him; and, my soul,
be swift to bring
All thy sweetness and thy dearest for the
triumph of our King!

593

Ruth Lake
© 1972 Scripture in Song / Thankyou Music

Therefore the redeemed of the Lord
shall return
And come with singing unto Zion,
And everlasting joy shall be upon their
head.

Therefore the redeemed of the Lord shall
return
And come with singing unto Zion,
And everlasting joy shall be upon their
head.

They shall obtain gladness and joy,
And sorrow and mourning shall flee away.
Therefore the redeemed of the Lord shall
return
And come with singing unto Zion,
And everlasting joy shall be upon their
head.

594

Joan Parsons
© 1978 Thankyou Music

1 **There is no condemnation for those who**
are in Christ,
For the Spirit of life in Christ has set me
free.

O He's alive, He's alive, He's alive,
O He's alive, He's alive, He's alive,
Praise the Lord.

2 If the Spirit of Him who raised Christ from
the dead
Be born in you, then He will give you life.
O He's alive, . . .

3 If God be for us, who can be against us?
For He who sent His Son will freely give us
all things.
O He's alive, . . .

They will run and not grow weary,
They will walk and not be faint.
Those whose hope is in the Lord
Shall renew their strength.

595 © Michael Saward, b. 1932

1 **These are the facts as we have received them,**
These are the truths that the Christian
believes,
This is the basis of all of our preaching:
Christ died for sinners and rose from the
tomb.

2 These are the facts as we have received
them:
Christ has fulfilled what the scriptures
foretold,
Adam's whole family in death had been
sleeping,
Christ through His rising restores us to life.

3 These are the facts as we have received
them:
We, with our Saviour, have died on the
cross;
Now, having risen, our Jesus lives in us,
Gives us His Spirit and makes us His home.

4 These are the facts as we have received
them:
We shall be changed in the blink of an eye,
Trumpets shall sound as we face life
immortal,
This is the victory through Jesus our Lord.

5 These are the facts as we have received
them,
These are the truths that the Christian
believes,
This is the basis of all of our preaching:
Christ died for sinners and rose from the
tomb.

596 © 1987 Andy Silver

They that wait upon the Lord
Shall renew their strength and mount on
eagles wings.
They that wait upon the Lord
Shall renew their strength and mount on
eagles wings.

597 © 1987 Greg Leavers

1 **This is what our Saviour said,**
He will return to the earth in power,
Coming on the clouds from heaven
All earth shall see Him and bow before Him.
He is the Alpha and Omega,
Who is and who was and who is to come;
Once He was dead and behold He now is
Living for evermore.

2 With a shout and trumpet sound
He'll fetch His bride for the marriage feast,
And then we'll see Him face to face,
Joining all heaven in praise and worship.
Blessing and glory and thanksgiving
Be to the Lamb reigning now and forever,
Honour and power belong to Jesus,
Come quickly Lord, Amen!

598 © 1987 Andy Silver

The heavens declare the glory of God,
And the heavens proclaim the work of His
hands,
And day after day they pour forth speech,
And night after night they display what He
knows.

599 Josiah Conder, 1789–1855

1 **Thou art the everlasting Word,**
The Father's only Son;
God manifestly seen and heard,
And Heaven's belovèd One:

Worthy, O Lamb of God, art Thou
That every knee to Thee should bow.

2 In Thee most perfectly expressed
The Father's glories shine;
Of the full Deity possessed,
Eternally Divine:
Worthy, O Lamb . . .

3 True image of the Infinite,
Whose essence is concealed;
Brightness of uncreated light,
The heart of God revealed:
Worthy, O Lamb . . .

4 But the high mysteries of Thy name
  An angel's grasp transcend;
  The Father only – glorious claim! –
  The Son can comprehend:
    Worthy, O Lamb . . .

5 Throughout the universe of bliss,
  The centre Thou, and sun;
  The eternal theme of praise is this,
  To Heaven's belovèd One:
    Worthy, O Lamb . . .

600
Dale Garratt
© 1979 Scripture in Song / Thankyou Music

Through our God we shall do valiantly,
It is He who will tread down our enemies.
We'll sing and shout His victory,
Christ is King!

For God has won the victory
And set His people free,
His word has slain the enemy,
The earth shall stand and see that
Through our God we shall do valiantly,
It is He who will tread down our enemies.

We'll sing and shout His victory,
Christ is King! Christ is King!
Christ is King!

601
Mary Peters, 1813–56

1 **Through the love of God our Saviour,**
  All will be well;
  Free and changeless is His favour,
  All, all is well:
  Precious is the blood that heals us,
  Perfect is the grace that seals us,
  Strong the hand stretched out to shield us,
  All must be well.

2 Though we pass through tribulation,
  All will be well;
  Ours is such a full salvation,
  All, all is well:
  Happy, still in God confiding,
  Fruitful, if in Christ abiding,
  Holy, through the Spirit's guiding,
  All must be well.

3 We expect a bright tomorrow,
  All will be well;
  Faith can sing, through days of sorrow,
  All, all is well:
  On our Father's love relying,
  Jesus every need supplying,
  Or in living or in dying,
  All must be well.

602
James E. Seddon, 1915–83
© Mavis Seddon / Jubilate Hymns

1 **To Him we come –**
  Jesus Christ our Lord,
  God's own living Word,
  His dear Son.
  In Him there is no east and west,
  In Him all nations shall be blessed;
  To all He offers peace and rest –
  Loving Lord!

2 In Him we live –
  Christ our strength and stay,
  Life and truth and way,
  Friend divine:
  His power can break the chains of sin,
  Still all life's storms without, within,
  Help us the daily fight to win –
  Living Lord!

3 For Him we go –
  Soldiers of the cross,
  Counting all things loss
  Him to know;
  Going to every land and race,
  Preaching to all redeeming grace,
  Building His church in every place –
  Conquering Lord!

4 With Him we serve –
  His the work we share
  With saints everywhere,
  Near and far;
  One in the task which faith requires,
  One in the zeal which never tires,
  One in the hope His love inspires –
  Coming Lord!

5 Onward we go –
  Faithful, bold, and true,
  Called His will to do
  Day by day
  Till, at the last, with joy we'll see
  Jesus, in glorious majesty;
  Live with Him through eternity –
  Reigning Lord!

603

© 1985 Andy Silver

To Him who is able to keep us,
To keep us from falling away,
Who'll bring us spotless and joyful
Into God's presence one day.
To the only God our Saviour,
Through Jesus Christ our Lord
Be glory, majesty, might and power,
Now, always – Amen.

604

Frances Ridley Havergal, 1836–79
Altered © 1987 Horrobin/Leavers

1 **True-hearted, whole-hearted! faithful
and loyal,**
King of our lives, by Your grace we'll stay
true!
Under Your standard, exalted and royal,
Strong in Your strength we will battle for
You!

*Peal out the watchword, and silence it
never,
Song of our spirits, rejoicing and free:
'True-hearted, whole-hearted, now and
for ever,
King of our lives, by Your grace we will
be.'*

2 True-hearted, whole-hearted! Fullest
allegiance
Yielding each day to our glorious King!
Valiant endeavour and loving obedience,
Freely and joyously now would we bring.
Peal out the . . .

3 True-hearted, Saviour, You know all our
story,
Weak are the hearts that we lay at Your feet;
Sinful and treacherous! Yet, for Your glory,
Heal them and cleanse them from sin and
deceit.
Peal out the . . .

4 True-hearted, whole-hearted! Saviour,
all-glorious,
Take Your great power and You reign
alone,
Over our wills and affections victorious –
Freely surrendered and wholly Your own.
Peal out the . . .

605

George Washington Doane, 1799–1859

1 **Thou art the Way, to Thee alone**
From sin and death we flee:
And he who would the Father seek
Must seek Him, Lord, by Thee.

2 Thou art the Truth, Thy word alone
True wisdom can impart;
Thou only canst inform the mind,
And purify the heart.

3 Thou art the Life, the rending tomb
Proclaims Thy conquering arm:
And those who put their trust in Thee
Nor death nor hell shall harm.

4 Thou art the Way, the Truth, the Life;
Grant us that Way to know,
That Truth to keep, that Life to win
Whose joys eternal flow.

606

German (15th cent.)
tr. Percy Dearmer, 1867–1936

1 **Unto us a Boy is born!**
King of all creation,
Came He to a world forlorn
The Lord of every nation,
The Lord of every nation.

2 Cradled in a stall was He
With sleepy cows and asses;
But the very beasts could see
That He all men surpasses,
That He all men surpasses.

3 Herod then with fear was filled:
'A Prince,' he said, 'in Jewry!'
All the little boys he killed
At Bethlehem in his fury,
At Bethlehem in his fury.

4 Now may Mary's Son, who came
So long ago to love us,
Lead us all with hearts aflame
Unto the joys above us,
Unto the joys above us.

5 Alpha and Omega He!
Let the organ thunder,
While the choir with peals of glee
Doth rend the air asunder!
Doth rend the air asunder!

607

David J. Hadden
© 1981 Springtide / Word Music (UK)

We are a chosen people,
A royal priesthood,
A holy nation belonging to God

1 You have called us out of darkness
To declare Your praise.
We exalt You and enthrone You.
Glorify Your name.
   We are a chosen . . .

2 You have placed us into Zion
In the new Jerusalem.
Thousand thousand are their voices,
Singing to the Lamb.
   We are a chosen . . .

608

Graham Kendrick
© 1985 Thankyou Music

1 **We are here to praise You,**
Lift our hearts and sing.
We are here to give You
The best that we can bring.

2 And it is our love rising from our hearts,
Ev'rything within us cries:
'Abba Father.'
Help us now to give You pleasure and
   delight,
Heart and mind and will that say:
'I love You Lord.'

609

Graham Kendrick
© 1985 Thankyou Music

1 **We are marching**
In the great procession,
Singers and dancers,
And musicians;
With the great congregation
We are moving onward,
Ever further and deeper
Into the heart of God.

   O give thanks to the Lord
   For His love will never end.

2 It's a march of victory,
It's a march of triumph,
Lifting Jesus higher
On a throne of praise.
With the banner of love
Flying over us
Ever further and deeper
Into the heart of God.
   O give thanks . . .

3 We will go to the nations
Spreading wide the fragrance
Of the knowledge of Jesus
Into every place.
Hear the great cloud of witnesses
Cheer us onward
Ever further and deeper
Into the heart of God.
   O give thanks . . .

4 And the whole creation
Waits in expectation
Of the full revelation
Of the sons of God;
As we march through history
To our blood-bought destiny
Ever further and deeper
Into the heart of God.

Ever further and deeper
Into the heart of God.

610

Ian Traynar
© 1977 Thankyou Music

1 **We are moving on into**
A deep appreciation
Of the love which flows from Father out
To ev'ry child of God,
Of the grace with which He handles
Ev'ry minute situation,
How He wants the best for ev'ryone
Who gives to Him his all.

   Grace it seems is all He has,
   And one big open heart;
   And it's so good
   Being loved by You, my Lord.

2 We will know and understand
His purposes more clearly,
O, the mystery of the things He does
In making us more whole.
With His love He woos us,
By His grace He sets us free;
We can only trust Him
And just hold on to His hand.
   Grace it seems . . .

611
Graham Kendrick
© 1986 Thankyou Music

1 **We believe in God the Father,**
Maker of the universe,
And in Christ His Son our saviour,
Come to us by virgin birth.
We believe He died to save us,
Bore our sins was crucified.
Then from death He rose victorious,
Ascended to the Father's side.

Jesus, Lord of all,
Lord of all, Jesus, Lord of all,
Lord of all, Jesus, Lord of all,
Lord of all, Jesus, Lord of all.
Name above all names,
Name above all names.

2 We believe He sends His Spirit,
On His church with gifts of power.
God His word of truth affirming,
Sends us to the nations now.
He will come again in glory,
Judge the living and the dead.
Every knee shall bow before Him,
Then must every tongue confess.
Jesus, Lord of all, . . .

612
© 1981 Kirk Dearman / Zondervan Music

We bring the sacrifice of praise
Into the house of the Lord,
We bring the sacrifice of praise
Into the house of the Lord.
And we offer up to You
The sacrifices of thanksgiving,
And we offer up to You
The sacrifices of joy.

613
Timothy Dudley-Smith, b. 1926

1 **We come as guests invited**
When Jesus bids us dine,
His friends on earth united
To share the bread and wine;
The bread of life is broken,
The wine is freely poured,
For us, in solemn token
Of Christ our dying Lord.

2 We eat and drink, receiving
From Christ the grace we need,
And in our hearts believing
On Him by faith we feed;
With wonder and thanksgiving
For love that knows no end,
We find in Jesus living
Our ever-present Friend.

3 One Bread is ours for sharing,
One single fruitful Vine,
Our fellowship declaring
Renewed in bread and wine –
Renewed, sustained and given
By token, sign and word,
The pledge and seal of heaven,
The love of Christ our Lord.

614
Thomas Hornblower Gill, 1819–1906

1 **We come unto our father's God:**
Their Rock is our salvation:
The eternal arms, their dear abode,
We make our habitation:
We bring Thee, Lord, the praise they
brought;
We seek Thee as Thy saints have sought
In ev'ry generation.

2 The fire divine, their steps that led,
Still goeth bright before us;
The heav'nly shield, around them spread,
Is still high holden o'er us:
The grace those sinners that subdued,
The strength those weaklings that renewed,
Doth vanquish, doth restore us.

3 The cleaving sins that brought them low
Are still our souls oppressing;
The tears that their eyes did flow
Fall fast, our shame confessing;
As with Thee, Lord, prevailed their cry,
So now our prayer ascends on high,
And bringeth down Thy blessing.

4 Their joy unto their Lord we bring;
Their song to us descendeth:
The Spirit Who in them did sing
To us His music lendeth.
His song in them, in us, is one;
We raise it high, we send it on—
The song that never endeth!

5 Ye saints to come, take up the strain,
The same sweet theme endeavour!
Unbroken be the golden chain,
Keep on the song for ever!
Safe in the same dear dwelling-place,
Rich with the same eternal grace,
Bless the same boundless Giver!

615 Mimi Farra
© 1975 Celebration / Thankyou Music

We cry, 'Hosanna, Lord,'
Yes, 'Hosanna, Lord,'
Yes, 'Hosanna, Lord,' to You.
We cry, 'Hosanna, Lord,'
Yes, 'Hosanna, Lord,'
Yes, 'Hosanna, Lord,' to You.

1 Behold, our Saviour comes.
Behold the Son of our God.
He offers Himself and He comes among us,
A lowly servant to all.
We cry, 'Hosanna, Lord,' . . .

2 Children wave their palms as the
King of all kings rides by.
Should we forget to praise our God,
The very stones would sing.
We cry, 'Hosanna, Lord,' . . .

3 He comes to set us free.
He gives us liberty.
His victory over death is th'eternal sign
Of God's love for us.
We cry, 'Hosanna, Lord,' . . .

616 Malcolm du Plessis
© 1984 Thankyou Music

We declare Your majesty,
We proclaim that Your name is exalted;
For You reign magnificently, rule
    victoriously,
And Your power is shown throughout the
    earth.

And we exclaim our God is mighty,
Lift up Your name, for You are holy.
Sing it again, all honour and glory,
In adoration we bow before Your throne.

617 © E.J. Burns, b. 1938

1 **We have a gospel to proclaim,**
Good news for men in all the earth;
The gospel of a saviour's name:
We sing His glory, tell His worth.

2 Tell of His birth at Bethlehem,
Not in a royal house or hall
But in a stable dark and dim:
The Word made flesh, a light for all.

3 Tell of His death at Calvary,
Hated by those He came to save;
In lonely suffering on the cross
For all He loved, His life He gave.

4 Tell of that glorious Easter morn:
Empty the tomb, for He was free;
He broke the power of death and hell
That we might share His victory.

5 Tell of His reign at God's right hand,
By all creation glorified;
He sends His Spirit on His church
To live for Him, the Lamb who died.

6 Now we rejoice to name Him king:
Jesus is Lord of all the earth;
This gospel-message we proclaim:
We sing His glory, tell His worth.

618 William Bullock, 1798–1874

1 **We love the place, O God,**
Wherein Thine honour dwells;
The joy of Thine abode
All earthly joy excels.

2 It is the house of prayer,
Wherein Thy servants meet;
And Thou, O Lord, art there,
Thy chosen flock to greet.

3 We love the word of life,
The word that tells of peace,
Of comfort in the strife,
And joys that never cease.

4 We love to sing below
Of mercies freely given;
But O we long to know
The triumph song of heaven!

5 Lord Jesus, give us grace,
On earth to love Thee more,
In heaven to see Thy face,
And with Thy saints adore.

619 Matthias Claudius, 1740–1815
tr. Jane Montgomery Campbell, 1817–78
Altered © 1986 Horrobin/Leavers

1 **We plough the fields and scatter**
The good seed on the land,
But it is fed and watered
By God's almighty hand;
He sends the snow in winter,
The warmth to swell the grain,
The breezes and the sunshine
And soft refreshing rain.

All good gifts around us
Are sent from heaven above,
Then thank the Lord, O thank the Lord,
For all His love.

2 He only is the Maker
Of all things near and far;
He paints the wayside flower,
He lights the evening star;
The wind and waves obey Him,
By Him the birds are fed;
Much more to us, His children,
He gives our daily bread.
    All good gifts . . .

3 We thank You then, O Father,
For all things bright and good,
The seed-time and the harvest,
Our life, our health, our food.
Accept the gifts we offer
For all Your love imparts,
We come now Lord to give You
Our humble, thankful hearts.
    All good gifts . . .

620 Fanny J. Crosby, 1823–1915
Altered © 1987 Horrobin/Leavers

1 **We praise You, we bless You, our
Saviour Divine,**
All power and dominion are yours for all
time!
We sing of Your mercy with joyful acclaim,
For You have redeemed us: all praise to
Your name!

2 All honour and praise to Your excellent
name,
Your love is unchanging – for ever the
same!
We bless and adore You, O Saviour and
King;
With joy and thanksgiving Your praises we
sing!

3 The strength of the hills and the depths of
the sea,
The earth and its fulness, Yours always shall
be,
And yet to the lowly You listen with care,
So ready their humble petitions to hear.

4 Your infinite goodness our tongues shall
employ;
You give to us richly all things to enjoy;
We'll follow Your footsteps, we'll rest in
Your love,
And soon we shall praise You in mansions
above!

621 Edith Gilling Cherry, 1872–97

1 **'We rest on Thee,' our Shield and our
Defender!**
We go not forth alone against the foe;
Strong in Thy strength, safe in Thy keeping
tender,
'We rest on Thee, and in Thy name we go.'
Strong in Thy strength, safe in Thy keeping
tender,
'We rest on Thee, and in Thy name we go.'

2 Yes, 'in Thy name,' O captain of salvation!
In Thy dear Name, all other names above;
Jesus our Righteousness, our sure
Foundation,
Our Prince of glory and our King of love.
Jesus our Righteousness, our sure
Foundation.
Our Prince of glory and our King of love.

3 We go in faith, our own great weakness
feeling,
And needing more each day Thy grace to
know:
Yet from our hearts a song of triumph
pealing;
'We rest on Thee, and in Thy name we go.'
Yet from our hearts a song of triumph
pealing.
'We rest on Thee, and in Thy name we go.'

4 'We rest on Thee,' our Shield and our
Defender!
Thine is the battle, Thine shall be the praise;
When passing through the gates of pearly
splendour,
Victors – we rest with Thee, through
endless days.
When passing through the gates of pearly
splendour,
Victors – we rest with Thee, through
endless days.

622 J.H. Hopkins Jnr., d. 1891
Altered © 1986 Horrobin/Leavers

1 **We three kings of Orient are;**
Bearing gifts we travel afar,
Field and fountain, moor and mountain,
Following yonder star:

    *O star of wonder, star of night,
    Star with royal beauty bright,
    Westward leading, still proceeding,
    Guide us to the perfect light.*

2 Born a King on Bethlehem plain,
   Gold I bring, to crown Him again –
   King for ever, ceasing never,
   Over us all to reign:
   O star of wonder . . .

3 Frankincense for Jesus have I,
   God on earth yet Priest on high;
   Prayer and praising all men raising
   Worship is earth's reply.
   O star of wonder . . .

4 Myrrh is mine; its bitter perfume
   Tells of His death and Calvary's gloom;
   Sorrowing, sighing, bleeding, dying,
   Sealed in a stone-cold tomb:
   O star of wonder . . .

5 Glorious now, behold Him arise,
   King, and God, and sacrifice:
   Heaven sings out 'Alleluia',
   'Amen' the earth replies:
   O star of wonder . . .

623 Copyright control

1 **Were you there when they crucified my
   Lord?**
   Were you there when they crucified my
   Lord?
   Oh! Sometimes it causes me to tremble,
   tremble, tremble:
   Were you there when they crucified my
   Lord?

2 Were you there when they nailed Him to the
   tree?
   Were you there when they nailed Him to the
   tree?
   Oh! Sometimes it causes me to tremble,
   tremble, tremble:
   Were you there when they nailed Him to the
   tree?

3 Were you there when they laid Him in the
   tomb?
   Were you there when they laid Him in the
   tomb?
   Oh! Sometimes it causes me to tremble,
   tremble, tremble:
   Were you there when they laid Him in the
   tomb?

4 Were you there when God raised Him from
   the dead?
   Were you there when God raised Him from
   the dead?
   Oh! Sometimes it causes me to tremble,
   tremble, tremble:
   Were you there when God raised Him from
   the dead?

624 William Chatterton Dix, 1837–98

1 **What Child is this, Who, laid to rest,**
   On Mary's lap is sleeping?
   Whom angels greet with anthems sweet,
   While shepherds watch are keeping?

   This, this is Christ the King,
   Whom shepherds guard and angels sing:
   Haste, haste to bring Him praise,
   The Babe, the Son of Mary.

2 Why lies He in such mean estate
   Where ox and ass are feeding?
   Good Christian fear: for sinners here
   The silent Word is pleading.
   This, this is Christ . . .

3 So bring Him incense, gold, and myrrh,
   Come, peasant, king, to own Him.
   The King of kings salvation brings,
   Let loving hearts enthrone Him.
   This, this is Christ . . .

625 Sue Read
© 1985 Thankyou Music

1 **When He comes we'll see just a child,**
   No warrior Lord but a baby so mild.
   The Lord says: 'Bethlehem though you are
   but small,
   In you shall be born the King.'
   When He comes, when He comes.

2 When He comes His reign shall bring
   peace,
   When He comes all fighting shall cease.
   Men shall hammer their spears into pruning
   hooks
   And prepare for battle no more.
   When He comes, when He comes.

   And on that day there will be laughter,
   On that day joy ever after, no more tears
   For the Lord will wipe them all away.
   And on that day, men shall be brothers,
   Reconciled to God and each other,
   The world shall see the King in His glory,
   When He comes.

3 When He comes He'll be of David's line,
The mighty God and ruler divine.
They'll call Him Wonderful and Counsellor,
And His kingdom shall never cease
When He comes, when He comes.
And on that day . . .

626 Copyright control

When I look into Your holiness,
When I gaze into Your loveliness,
When all things that surround
Become shadows in the light of You.

When I've found the joy of reaching Your
 heart,
When my will becomes enthroned in Your
 love,
When all things that surround
Become shadows in the light of You.

I worship You, I worship You.
The reason I live is to worship You.
I worship You, I worship You.
The reason I live is to worship You.

627 © 1977 Timothy Dudley-Smith, b. 1926

1 **When to our world the Saviour came**
The sick and helpless heard His name,
And in their weakness longed to see
The healing Christ of Galilee.

2 That good physician! night and day
The people thronged about His way;
And wonder ran from soul to soul –
'The touch of Christ has made us whole!'

3 His praises then were heard and sung
By opened ears and loosened tongue,
While lightened eyes could see and know
The healing Christ of long ago.

4 Of long ago – yet living still.
Who died for us on Calvary's hill;
Who triumphed over cross and grave,
His healing hands stretched forth to save.

5 Those wounded hands are still the same,
And all who serve that saving Name
May share today in Jesus' plan –
The healing Christ of everyman.

6 Then, grant us, Lord, in this our day,
To hear the prayers the helpless pray;
Give to us hearts their pain to share,
Make of us hands to tend and care.

7 Make us your hands! For Christ to live,
In prayer and service, swift to give;
Till all the world rejoice to find
The healing Christ of all mankind.

628 © Timothy Dudley-Smith, b. 1926

1 **When the Lord in glory comes**
Not the trumpets, not the drums,
Not the anthem, not the psalm,
Not the thunder, not the calm,
Not the shout the heavens raise,
Not the chorus, not the praise,
Not the silences sublime,
Not the sounds of space and time,
But His voice when He appears
Shall be music to my ears—
But His voice when He appears
Shall be music to my ears.

2 When the Lord is seen again
Not the glories of His reign,
Not the lightnings through the storm,
Not the radiance of His form,
Not His pomp and power alone,
Not the splendours of His throne,
Not His robe and diadems,
Not the gold and not the gems,
But His face upon my sight
Shall be darkness into light—
But His face upon my sight
Shall be darkness into light.

3 When the Lord to human eyes
Shall bestride our narrow skies,
Not the child of humble birth,
Not the carpenter of earth,
Not the man by all denied,
Not the victim crucified,
But the God who died to save,
But the victor of the grave,
He it is to whom I fall,
Jesus Christ, my All in all—
He it is to whom I fall,
Jesus Christ, my All in all.

629 Nahum Tate, 1652–1715

1 **While shepherds watched their flocks
 by night,**
All seated on the ground,
The angel of the Lord came down,
And glory shone around:

2 'Fear not!' said he (for mighty dread
   Had seized their troubled mind)
   'Glad tidings of great joy I bring
   To you and all mankind.

3 'To you in David's town, this day
   Is born, of David's line,
   A Saviour, who is Christ the Lord;
   And this shall be the sign:

4 'The heavenly babe you there shall find
   To human view displayed.
   All meanly wrapped in swaddling bands,
   And in a manger laid.'

5 Thus spake the angel; and forthwith
   Appeared a shining throng
   Of angels, praising God, who thus
   Addressed their joyful song:

6 'All glory be to God on high,
   And to the earth be peace;
   Goodwill henceforth from heaven to men
   Begin and never cease.'

630
Based on the book of Nahum
© 1987 Anne Horrobin & Sue Cartwright

Where the Lord walks, storms arise,
The clouds are the dust raised by His feet,
The earth shakes when the Lord appears,
The world and its people tremble.

1 You, Nineveh, are a wicked city,
   Your people plot against me,
   You've made my people Israel suffer,
   But now I'm going to set them free.
   Where the Lord walks . . .

2 The Lord will always protect His people,
   He'll care for those who trust Him,
   But turn against Him, oppose the Lord,
   And His judgement then is death.
   Where the Lord walks . . .

3 I say to my people Israel,
   A messenger is bringing good news,
   Stand in the victory I've given you,
   For your enemy has been destroyed.
   Where the Lord walks . . .

631
Jane and Betsy Clowe
© 1974, 1975 Celebration / Thankyou Music

Wind, Wind blow on me;
Wind, Wind set me free!
Wind, Wind my Father sent
The blessèd Holy Spirit.

1 Jesus told us all about You,
   How we could not live without You,
   With His blood the power bought
   To help us live the life He taught.
   Wind, Wind . . .

2 When we're weary You console us,
   When we're lonely You enfold us,
   When in danger You uphold us,
   Blessèd Holy Spirit.
   Wind, Wind . . .

3 When into the church You came,
   It was not in Your own but Jesus' name:
   Jesus Christ is still the same—
   He sends the Holy Spirit.
   Wind, Wind . . .

4 Set us free to love our brothers,
   Set us free to live for others,
   That the world the Son might see
   And Jesus' name exalted be.
   Wind, Wind . . .

632
Arthur Tappan Pierson, 1837–1911

1 **With harps and with viols there stand a
   great throng**
   In the presence of Jesus, and sing this new
   song:

   *Unto Him Who has loved us and washed
   us from sin,*
   Unto Him be the glory for ever! Amen.

2 All these once were sinners, defiled in His
   sight,
   Now arrayed in pure garments in praise
   they unite:
   Unto Him Who has . . .

3 He's made of the rebel a priest and a king,
   He has bought us, and taught us this new
   song to sing:
   Unto Him Who has . . .

4 How helpless and hopeless we sinners had
   been,
   If He never had loved us till cleansed from
   our sin!
   Unto Him Who has . . .

5 Aloud in His praises our voices shall ring,
   So that others, believing, this new song shall
        sing:
   Unto Him Who has . . .

633 Paul Armstrong
© 1980 Springtide / Word Music (UK)

1 **Wonderful Counsellor,**
   The Mighty God,
   The Everlasting Father,
   The Prince of Peace,
   The Prince of Peace,
   The Everlasting Father,
   The Mighty God.

2 Wonderful Counsellor,
   Wonderful Counsellor,
   Wonderful is the name of Jesus,
   Wonderful Counsellor,
   Wonderful Counsellor,
   Wonderful is the name of Jesus.

634 © 1980 Norman Warren

1 **With my heart I worship You Jesus,**
   Jesus;
   With my heart I worship You Jesus, Jesus:
   You gave all in love for me,
   Saved me for eternity;
   With my heart I worship You.

   ALTERNATIVE VERSES:

   With my lips I praise You . . .

   With my life I serve You . . .

635 David J. Hadden
© 1983 Restoration Music Ltd

Worthy is the Lamb seated on the
   throne,
   Worthy is the Lamb who was slain,
   To receive power and riches,
   And wisdom and strength,
   Honour and glory,
   Glory and praise,
   For ever and evermore.

636 Mark S. Kinzer
© 1976, 1980 The Word of God

Worthy, O worthy are You Lord,
Worthy to be thank'd and prais'd
And worshipp'd and ador'd.
Worthy, O worthy are You Lord,
Worthy to be thank'd and prais'd
And worshipp'd and ador'd.

Singing Hallelujah,
Lamb upon the throne,
We worship and adore You,
Make Your glory known.
Hallelujah,
Glory to the King:
You're more than a conqueror,
You're Lord of ev'rything.

637 Richard Baxter, 1615–91
alt. John Hampden Gurney, 1802–62
and Richard Robert Chopf, 1830–1928

1 **Ye holy angels bright,**
   Who wait at God's right hand,
   Or through the realms of light
   Fly at your Lord's command,
   Assist our song,
   Or else the theme
   Too high doth seem
   For mortal tongue.

2 Ye blessèd souls at rest,
   Who see your Saviour's face,
   Whose glory, e'en the least
   Is far above our grace,
   God's praises sound,
   As in His sight
   With sweet delight
   Ye do abound.

3 Ye saints, who toil below,
   Adore your heavenly King,
   And onward as ye go,
   Some joyful anthem sing;
   Take what He gives,
   And praise Him still
   Through good and ill,
   Who ever lives.

4 My soul, bear thou thy part,
   Triumph in God above,
   And with a well-tuned heart
   Sing thou the songs of love.
   Let all the days
   Till life shall end,
   Whate'er He send,
   Be filled with praise.

638 © 1984 Colin Preston

Yes, power belongs to You, O Lord,
In You we put our trust,
You are sovereign over all,
Great are You.
Great in Your mercy, Lord,
Great in Your love,
A mighty warrior in whom we trust.
Glorify Your name,
Glorify Your name, glorify Your name.

Don't worry about the opposition,
For I stand with the few,
The proud, the violent godless man
Will know I stand with you.
   Yes, power belongs . . .

Do not fear nor be dismayed,
The battle is not yours,
You shall not need to fight, but stand
And see salvation of the Lord.
   Yes, power belongs . . .

Be still and know that I am God,
And wait upon My word,
Responding to My Spirit's voice,
With your breath and praise do war.
   Yes, power belongs . . .

639
Frances Ridley Havergal, 1836–79
Altered © 1986 Horrobin/Leavers

You are coming, O my Saviour,
You are coming, O my King;
In Your beauty all resplendent,
In Your glory all transcendent;
Well may we rejoice and sing.
Coming soon my living Lord,
Heralds sing Your glorious praise;
Coming! Now on earth adored,
Songs of triumph we shall raise.

You are coming, You are coming;
We shall meet You on Your way,
We shall see You, we shall see You,
We shall bless You, we shall show You
All our hearts could never say.
What an anthem that will be,
Ringing out eternally,
Earth's and heaven's praises meet,
At Your own all glorious feet!

3 O the joy to see You reigning,
You, my own beloved Lord!
Every tongue Your name confessing,
Worship, honour, glory blessing
Brought to You with glad accord –
You, my Master and my Friend,
Vindicated and enthroned,
Unto earth's remotest end
Glorified, adored, and owned!

640
John Hampden Gurney, 1802–1862

1 **Yes, God is good—in earth and sky,**
From ocean depths and spreading wood,
Ten thousand voices seem to cry:
God made us all, and God is good.

2 The sun that keeps His trackless way,
And downward pours His golden flood,
Night's sparkling hosts, all seem to say
In accents clear, that God is good.

3 The joyful birds prolong the strain,
Their song with every spring renewed;
The air we breathe, and falling rain,
Each softly whispers: God is good.

4 I hear it in the rushing breeze;
The hills that have for ages stood,
The echoing sky and roaring seas,
All swell the chorus: God is good.

5 Yes, God is good, all nature says,
By God's own hand with speech endued;
And man, in louder notes of praise,
Should sing for joy that God is good.

6 For all Your gifts we bless You Lord,
But chiefly for our heavenly food;
Your pardoning grace, Your quickening
   word,
These prompt our song, that God is good.

641
Michael Ledner
© 1981 Maranatha Music USA / Word Music (UK)

You are my hiding place,
You always fill my heart
With songs of deliverance
Whenever I am afraid.

I will trust in You,
I will trust in You,
Let the weak say
I am strong in the strength of my God.

642

Eddie Espinosa
© 1982 Mercy Music / Thankyou Music

1 **You are the Mighty King,**
The living Word;
Master of ev'rything,
You are the Lord.

And I praise Your name,
And I praise Your name.

2 You are Almighty God,
Saviour and Lord;
Wonderful Counsellor,
You are the Lord.

And I praise Your name,
And I praise Your name.

3 You are the Prince of Peace,
Emmanuel;
Everlasting Father,
You are the Lord.

And I love Your name,
And I love Your name.

4 You are the Mighty King,
The living Word;
Master of ev'rything,
You are the Lord.

643

Danny Daniels
© 1982 Mercy Music / Thankyou Music

You are the Vine, we are the branches,
Keep us abiding in You.
You are the Vine, we are the branches,
Keep us abiding in You.

Then we'll grow in Your love,
Then we'll go in Your name,
That the world will surely know
That You have power to heal and to save.

You are the Vine, we are the branches,
Keep us abiding in You.

644

Noel Richards
© 1985 Thankyou Music

You laid aside Your majesty,
Gave up ev'rything for me,
Suffer'd at the hands
Of those You had created.
You took all my guilt and shame,
When You died and rose again;
Now today You reign,
In heav'n and earth exalted.

I really want to worship You, my Lord,
You have won my heart and I am Yours
For ever and ever; I will love You.
You are the only one who died for me,
Gave Your life to set me free,
So I lift my voice to You in adoration.

645

Richard Taylor
© 1982 Springtide / Word Music (UK)

Your love is to me like an everflowing
   stream,
Your love is to me like an everflowing
   stream,
Your love is to me like an everflowing
   stream
Reaching out Lord.

Lord we need Your love,
Yes, we need Your love,
We need Your love to make it through;
Lord we need Your love,
Yes, we need Your love,
We need Your love to make it through.

646

John Daniel Lawtum
© 1982 Word Music (UK)

You are worthy, Lord,
You are worthy, so I lift my heart,
I lift my voice and cry 'Holy'.
You have sav'd me, and I love You,
Jesus evermore
I live to praise Your name.

647

Helen Thomas
© 1984 Thankyou Music

Yours, Lord, is the greatness,
The power, the glory.
Yours, Lord, is the greatness,
The victory, the majesty.

1 For everything in heaven and earth is
      Yours,
   You are the King, supreme over all.
      Yours, Lord . . .

2 All riches and honour come from You;
   You are our God, You make us strong.
      Yours, Lord . . .

3 And now, our God, we give You thanks,
   We praise Your glorious name.
      Yours, Lord . . .

Index of First Lines

Titles which differ from first lines are shown in italics